Take Action!

A GUIDE TO CITIZENSHIP

elburger

elburger

Contents

Acknowledgments

We would like to thank everyone who helped to make this book a reality, in particular the many young people in schools and in communities across Canada and the USA whose questions, ideas, and success stories convinced us of the importance of such a leadership manual for youth.

A special word of gratitude to Roxanne Joyal for her assistance on the first draft of the book, and for her unwavering dedication and support. As well, our appreciation goes out to Deepa Shankaran for her written contributions and to Kyle Kreiss, Erin Barton, Ed Gillis, and Sarah Kane who put the ideas into practice at our leadership training sessions for youth.

We would like to extend a special thank you to Janice Schoening, Nancy Christoffer, and the team at Gage Learning Corporation for believing in this project and for being so patient and understanding. Thanks also to reviewers Gregory T. G. Smith of Okanagan Similkameen School District, BC and Maria Volante of Niagara Catholic District School Board, ON.

Our work would not be possible without an encouraging and supportive group of adults and youth who believe in Kids Can Free The Children and Leaders Today activities. Thank you to the KCFTC staff and Board of Directors including Eva and Yoel Haller, Rowene Nutter, Sister Cathy, John Gaither, Fintan Kilbride, Lloyd Hanoman, Victor and Wendy Lee, Jonathan White, Shelley Krupski, Tanya Reda, Alison Cohen, Leonard Kurz, the Roman Family, Vivien Stewart, Maria Colavecchia, Susan Bardfield, Marion Stewart, Toinette Bezant, Malani Moorthy, Theresa Bonner, and all past and present KCFTC Board members, employees, and volunteers who enabled us to grow and engage thousands of young people from around the world.

Our gratitude goes to the organizations and individuals who believe in our important mission. In this respect we include Virginia and Shaw Benderly, David Krieger and the Nuclear Age Peace Foundation, Oprah Winfrey and the Angel Network, Tim Brodhead and the McConnell Foundation, Lekha Singh and the I-2 Foundation, the Threshold Foundation, Buzz Hargrove and the Canadian Auto Worker's Union, Kuki Gallmann and the Gallmann Memorial Foundation, The Illinois State Math and Science Academy including Stephanie Pace Marshall and Bob Hernandez, Glen McCall, the Kirsch family, and St. Mary's Church Pompton Lakes, Mary and Brigit Fednik, Michael McCarthy, Peter Ruhiu, Elaine Silver, Marion Stewart, the Apostolopoulos Family, and all of the youth members with whom we have worked.

Our family deserves a heart-felt thank you including our 88 year old Mimi who is our biggest fan, Norman Gagnon, Marcella Bonner, Pat and Dave Cappellani, and our mascot, Chip! Finally, and most importantly, we would not be who we are without the love and continuous support of our parents, Fred and Theresa Kielburger. Thank you for everything Mom and Dad, we love you!

A Message from Craig Kielburger

While eating breakfast one morning in Toronto, I reached for my favorite section of the newspaper, the comics. Suddenly, I noticed the picture of a boy on the front page of the paper. The headline read, "Battled Child Labor, Boy 12, Murdered!" Being 12 years old myself, I felt an immediate connection and grabbed the paper to read more.

I had never heard about child labor but decided to do some research. When I discovered that there were more than 250 million child laborers in the world, many working in slavelike conditions, I knew I had to do something. I was not sure how I could help, but I knew I had to at least try.

When I gathered my friends to start Kids Can Free the Children, we were simply a group of Canadian youth getting together to write letters, make phone calls, fundraise, and take other small actions on an issue we felt passionate about. At first, no one believed that children could actually make a difference. But they can. We proved it.

What started out as a group of kids dreaming about changing the world has, in six short years, grown into an influential international movement, involving over 100,000 youth in 35 countries, speaking out and taking action on behalf of their peers. The impact of Kids Can Free the Children has been remarkable. Through the efforts of young people, Kids Can Free the Children has been able to build and open over 300 primary schools in developing countries, providing education to over 15,000 children; ship over 100,000 school and health kits to developing countries; and pressure governments around the world to enact laws to protect children.

People sometimes ask me what type of person makes the best leader. My response: All types! Every one of us is born with special gifts or talents. And as young people, it is both our right and our responsibility to use these talents to help find solutions to problems affecting our world. The first thing we need to do is learn as much as possible about the issues that concern us as youth.

Young people are in a unique position to change the world. All we have to do is believe that we can make a difference, and we will.

We hope this book will help you use your special gifts to become a powerful force for progress and change.

> "Life's most urgent question is: What are you doing for others?"
>
> — Martin Luther King, Jr. (1929–1968) Civil rights leader

Craig Kielburger
Founder, Kids Can Free the Children
www.freethechildren.com

TAKE ACTION!

How to Use This Book

This book has been inspired by the vision, spirit, and activities of thousands of youth working to improve the lives of others in their schools and communities. Their ideas and actions have led to the formation of Leaders Today. Leaders Today is a global organization that trains young people to become socially involved on a local, national, or international level. It runs leadership training programs in schools, community centers, and places of worship, and leads workshops on educational topics such as how to give effective speeches, how to fundraise, and how to inspire others to become socially involved. Leaders Today also offers leadership training and volunteer programs in Kenya, India, Thailand, and Nicaragua, where young people from North America and Europe volunteer at Free the Children projects, help build primary schools, and make a real difference while working in a local community. (More information about Leaders Today is available at the back of this book.)

What has emerged out of the hundreds of Leaders Today training programs offered around the world each year is the realization that each one of us has the potential to change the world. It does not matter where you live or how old you are — your contributions are important and can help promote change. What young people often lack, however, are the tools to take action. This step-by-step guide to social action has been designed to show you how to get organized and get moving to tackle important issues in your community, your school, your country, and around the world.

"Young people are the leaders of tomorrow," or so the saying goes. But you do not have to wait until tomorrow to change the world. You can be a leader today, and *Take Action! A Guide to Active Citizenship* will show you how. By following the suggestions in this book, you will be taking concrete action and helping to make a difference in your life and in the lives of others.

Each of the five main parts of this book, described below, contains valuable tips, strategies, and examples that will help you to become more socially aware and involved.

Part 1: How to Get Involved: The Step-By-Step Process outlines seven steps to social involvement, which are easy-to-follow guidelines for developing personal skills while tackling a new social issue.

Part 2: The How-To Guide contains suggestions regarding communication, media, fundraising, and research that you will find invaluable when you decide to take action on your social issue.

Part 3: Where You Can Get Involved — Everywhere! will inspire you to become socially active at home, in your school, in your community, and by working with government.

Part 4: Tackling Social Issues provides information about seven social issues that need your help. Here, you learn about seven concrete plans of action, which you can follow to make a difference. You will also be introduced to a number of ordinary young people who have made an extraordinary impact on these issues.

Part 5: Sources and Resources lists the names of organizations working to make a difference, and provides current contact information (at the time of publication).

Here are some things to think about while reading this book:

• Think of this book as a springboard for new ideas and do not limit yourself to the plans it provides for social action. Be creative. Be original. Challenge yourself to come up with new ways to help. Being a leader means taking steps beyond what you thought was originally possible. It means believing in your power to change the world.

• Every time you tackle a new social issue, review the section Seven Steps to Social Involvement, beginning on page 2. By becoming more and more familiar with these steps, you will have a greater impact on your issue.

• Do not be afraid to ask for help. Many people want to make the world a better place in which to live, and both youth and adults alike are often looking for ways to make a contribution.

• Do not give up. Getting involved in social issues is difficult sometimes because learning about the world's problems can be depressing. But if you get frustrated, do not turn away; instead, turn to other people for support. Find out how others have conquered the odds and remind yourself why you got involved. Turn your anger and your passion into action.

Remember, we are the generation that we have been waiting for. Good luck!

Marc Kielburger

Marc Kielburger
Co-Founder, Leaders Today
www.leaderstoday.com

PART 1
How to Get Involved:
The Step-by-Step Process

Seven Steps to Social Involvement

Are you interested in becoming socially involved? Have you come across a social issue that motivates you but you are uncertain about where to start? You are not alone. It is often very difficult to become socially active. Many of the problems currently facing the world, such as child labor, AIDS, or war and conflict, are complicated and controversial. However, simply because an issue is difficult does not mean you should avoid becoming involved in it. Frequently, the more complex the issue, the more your help is needed. This section of the book introduces you to seven easy steps you can take to break down the issue into manageable stages for your social involvement. Following the suggestions outlined for each step will help you become a more effective social advocate. Try to use these seven steps every time you pick a new issue in which to become active. Doing so will maximize the impact of your involvement.

Step 1: Choose an Issue

The first and most important step in becoming socially involved is to choose an issue that you are passionate about. Ask yourself: What social problem motivates and inspires me? Try to find a topic that you would like to research in order to learn as much as you can.

There are so many ways that you can make a difference. What issues are important to you?

Be observant and ask questions

Is there something in the world that does not seem fair or just to you? Perhaps you have read about it in a newspaper or on the Internet, or seen it on television. Is there anything that you would like to change at school, in your community, or in the world?

When choosing your issue, try to be as specific as possible. If your issue is, for example, war and conflict, try to focus on one particular aspect of that topic. You could become involved in ridding the world of nuclear weapons or addressing the problem of child soldiers in Sierra Leone. The chart below lists other examples.

Once you have chosen your issue, find out what other organized groups are already addressing this or associated issues. Thoroughly research the groups to make sure they are legitimate and credible, and then consider approaching them for help. You may also want to research to determine how other individuals and groups are making significant contributions in your community.

Issue	Specific Problem
world hunger	Students at my school are hungry.
	Children in North Korea are starving.
child labor	A local store is importing clothes made in sweatshops that use child labor.
war and conflict	Some countries harbor and finance terrorists.
	Many war criminals are not brought to justice.
poverty	Our city lacks shelters for the hundreds of homeless people.
	One in six children in the United States lives in poverty.
AIDS	Millions of people in sub-Saharan Africa are dying from AIDS.
	People in our community have the illness and need our help.

Step 2: Do Your Research

It is important to learn more about the problems that prevent millions of people around the world from being healthy, happy, and reaching their full potential. If you want to help them have a better life, you have to educate yourself. You have to know what you are fighting for.

What is the best way to start your research?

Read newspapers and magazines to keep up-to-date on current events. Then visit the library to learn more about the topics that sparked your interest. If an issue is too large to learn about all at once, remember to break it down into several smaller issues and think about the different aspects of each problem. This will make your research more manageable.

Begin by determining what specific issues are related to your topic. For example:

Poverty ⟶ Issues related to poverty

- unemployment
- hunger
- child labor
- homelessness
- disease

Where can you obtain information?

- Library
- Textbooks
- Internet
- Teachers, principal, parents/guardians, and community leaders
- News media
- Government
- Surveys and interviews
- Organizations and community groups
- Corporations and local businesses
- Magazines and newspapers
- Films

Begin your research by making a list of specific questions concerning the issue, and then set out to answer them. To gain a broader understanding of the problem you are researching, think about its causes, its consequences, and its possible solutions.

Example issue: Child labor

Here are some questions you might ask yourself:

Causes

- What is child labor?
- Why are children working? Examine all the causes.

- What situations force children into child labor?
- Where are they working? In which countries is child labor extensive? What kinds of industries employ children?

Consequences

- How many children are working?
- What kind of work do they do? What are the dangers involved in child labor?
- Is all work harmful to children?
- Are there any advantages to child labor?
- Who is benefiting from child labor?
- What are the long-term effects on children and on society?

Solutions

- What is being done to solve the problem? What does and does not work?
- Who are the decision-makers I need to approach in order to solve the problem?
- What laws are in effect in various countries to protect children? Are additional laws needed?
- What can I do to help children who are exploited in child labor?

> " You gain strength, courage, and confidence by every experience in which you really stop to look fear in the face.... You must do the thing you think you cannot do. "
>
> — Eleanor Roosevelt (1884–1962) Former First Lady, United States

Researching made easy

Tip 1: Choose a direction

Before diving into your research, consider what the information will be used for: a fundraising campaign, a speech, a report, an information display, a flyer or pamphlet. This will give you an idea of the kind of material you are looking for, as well as how much research information you will need for your project.

Tip 2: Set a goal and a deadline

Set a goal for each study session. Know what you want to accomplish and give yourself a deadline. For example, tell yourself that you will read and take notes on three one-page newspaper articles in one hour.

Try to set a reasonable goal, one that you will be able to reach if you work hard. That way, you will finish your study session feeling great about yourself and the work you have done.

Tip 3: Tackle one thing at a time

In your reading, you might come across other topics that spark your interest. Do some investigating, explore, and then make a note to return to them later to dig deeper, but try to stay focused on the task at hand. It is easier to concentrate and more will be accomplished if you focus on only a few things at one time.

Tip 4: Organize your information

As you conduct research, you will need to organize the information you obtain. You may wish to use such methods as summaries, notes, timelines, visual organizers, maps, or comparison organizers. Make sure that the method you choose suits the information you are trying to organize, and remember to accurately document your sources of information.

Tip 5: Get others involved

Is there too much to do? If so, make the research task a group project. Research is a great way to get others interested and involved in your cause. Divide up your issue into different subjects and have each group member take ownership of one of the subjects. After some initial research, share what you have learned with the group. This way, you will all gain a more complete understanding of the issue.

Tip 6: Ask the experts

Contact organizations that are devoted to the issue you are researching. They can direct you to reliable resources and provide you with some information to get started. (See Part 5 for contact information that may help you.)

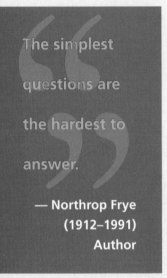

> The simplest questions are the hardest to answer.
>
> — Northrop Frye
> (1912–1991)
> Author

How to Be a Critical Reader

Do not believe everything you read

When doing research, it is important to compare different sources before you accept as true what one book says. Do not be impressed by words just because they are in print. Be critical of information. Books are not always accurate; sometimes their statistics are outdated or incorrect. The numbers you find might either be reduced or exaggerated, depending on how the writer wants you to react. If you have information from a variety of sources, compare the material to see if the sources agree and the numbers match up. If they do not, then you have some investigating to do.

Beware of bias

Whether or not they are conscious of it, all writers have a different point of view, also known as bias. The way they grew up and the experiences they have had have shaped their perception and interpretation of the world around them.

In order to determine the bias contained in the material you are reading, consider the following:

✔ **Author:** Who is the author? What kind of education or experience has this person had? Is she or he an expert on the subject? From what political, social, and economic position is this author writing?

✔ **Audience:** For whom was this article intended?

✔ **Intent:** Why was this article written? What main point is the author trying to convince you of?

Consider both sides of the issue

Once you start reading, chances are you will uncover many interesting facts, but some might surprise or shock you. So before you get carried away, make sure you have the whole story. Researching a topic means looking at both sides of the issue. This is the only way to get a clear, unbiased understanding of what is really going on. It is important to consider both the positive and the negative aspects of the issue before forming an opinion. Doing so will help you to devise more effective solutions and will make your argument stronger when you are ready to take a stand.

Documentation: Know your source

Because you are young, some people will challenge your facts. If this happens, demonstrate that you have done your homework.

As you research, write down all the bibliographical information about your sources. Check the references cited or the bibliography of your source to find out where the author obtained his or her information. Make sure that your information is coming from an informed and reliable source and that your notes are accurate.

If you can support your statements with solid facts, you will be confident in sharing what you have learned.

The Internet as a research tool

The Internet puts an unlimited amount of information at your fingertips, but how reliable is it all? The fact is, anyone can have a site on the Internet. There are often no editors and no supervisors, no one to make sure that what is floating around in cyberspace is true. The trick to doing research on the Internet is to learn to distinguish between fact and opinion, and to confirm the information you find. Think of the Internet as one resource, not the only resource.

What can you rely on?

Generally speaking, you can assume that the information contained on a Web site set up by a university, government, or major institution is reliable. Because they have a reputation to uphold, these sources usually make sure that the information they post is accurate. But keep in mind that every organization has its own agenda, so it is always best to check more than one source when you are doing your research.

A Checklist for the Wise Web Researcher

Who's behind the scenes?

✔ Are the authors of the site identified?

✔ What qualifications do they have?

✔ What kind of professional or institutional associations do the authors have?

✔ Is there an email address that you can use to contact the authors and ask questions?

✔ Are there links to reliable sites where the accuracy of the information can be confirmed?

Is the site up-to-date?

✔ Is there a date when the site was last updated?

✔ If so, has the information been revised recently?

Documentation and accuracy

✔ Are there references or a bibliography to verify that the information is true?

✔ Does the site credit the sources of its information? (A reliable source states clearly where the information originated.)

✔ Based on the research you have already done, does the information on the site seem accurate?

Intention

✔ What is the goal of the site? What is it trying to convince you of?

✔ Can you sense a bias in the visual or written material?

✔ Is a stereotype being promoted?

Language

✔ Is the language professional and appropriate?

✔ Does the site use proper grammar, spelling, and punctuation?

Step 3: Build a Team

Tell others about your issue and ask if they want to help. When people see you are sincere about your area of concern, and hear you explain why it is important to help, some of them will want to get involved. These people will be your teammates and you will grow to rely on their support, advice, and ideas. Remember, any successful team respects the rights and opinions of all its members.

How to get others involved

Concerned that no one will want to join your team and become involved in a social issue that needs change? Here are some strategies for motivating others to become active and socially committed:

Talk to...

✔ your family and friends
✔ people in your school and community
✔ your teachers and principal

Seek permission to hold an information presentation...

✔ for students in your class and school
✔ at your local church, synagogue, temple, mosque, or other place of worship
✔ at community gatherings
✔ at sports clubs in which you are involved

Promote the issue by...

✔ hosting a party
✔ putting on a play
✔ organizing an exhibit
✔ hosting a sporting event
✔ distributing flyers at school or in the community

Exercise strong team leadership by...

✔ understanding and celebrating differences among team members
✔ welcoming everyone's contribution
✔ utilizing individual talents
✔ building a team that is representative of various cultures and communities
✔ identifying what else can be done to get others involved

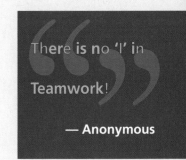

There is no 'I' in Teamwork!

— Anonymous

How to Get Involved: The Step-by-Step Process

9

Step 4: Call a Meeting

Once you have a group of people who are interested in your cause, it is time to call a formal meeting. (See Part 2 for more information on how to hold a meeting.)

You may find that holding your first meeting is a difficult task, but take heart. Organizing effective and efficient meetings takes a lot of practice. Here are some points to keep in mind when you organize your first meeting:

Find a place to hold the meeting

Where will your meeting be held? Will you need to seek permission to hold the meeting? Some possible meeting places include

- home
- school
- hall or place of worship
- community center
- local library
- restaurant

Tip

At the meeting, it is crucial that all of your teammates understand the issue. Encourage members of the team to research and then share what they have discovered with others at the meeting. This will enhance everyone's understanding of the issue.

Set an agenda for the meeting

- Have a definite purpose in mind for the meeting.
- Outline the points to be discussed.

- Prepare written material/ information for presentation to the group. (See Part 2 for more information on agendas.)

Conduct the meeting

- Thank everyone for coming.
- Outline the purpose of the meeting.
- Have someone take notes or record on audiotape what is said.
- Discuss what you have learned from your research.
- Make a plan of action with the group.

Conclude the meeting

- Set a date for a second meeting.
- Establish where the next meeting will be held.
- Discuss the purpose of the next meeting.
- Ask for help with organizing the next meeting.

Step 5: Make a Plan of Action

Making a plan of action is often one of the most exciting steps. Your action plan will be your guide and compass to making a difference. How do you make a plan of action? By brainstorming! Come up with creative, crazy, and fun ideas and ways to positively affect your issue.

Here are a few brainstorming tips:

✔ Identify a recorder to write down all the ideas.

✔ Allow enough time for every team member to talk.

✔ Listen attentively.

✔ Be positive. Everyone's ideas have value.

✔ Be creative. All ideas have potential.

In your first brainstorming session, you may want to do the following:

1. Define your goal: What does your group hope to accomplish?

It is helpful for the group to have a mandate. A mandate is a statement that describes the purpose of the group. Here are two examples of mandates for groups of young people who are concerned about child poverty:

"Our mandate is to hold a food drive to collect items for the local food bank so poor kids in our community will not have to be hungry."

"Our mandate is to get the school board to provide a breakfast program to needy students in all the schools in our district so no kid has to go to class hungry."

2. List the names of those people who will be helpful and those who might oppose your action.

• Who has the power and the authority to make the changes you want?

• How can adults help?

• Who will oppose your idea? Why?

• How will you address opposition?

3. Develop a strategy.

- How much time can the members give to the cause?

- What responsibility will each person have?

- What role will adults play? (Although adults can play an important role, do not let adults take over your group. Remember, you are a youth organization.)

4. Create a message or logo for your cause.

- Develop a youth-friendly and fun logo with lots of color. For example, the Leaders Today logo depicts an artistic interpretation of a person speaking at a podium. It is simple, fun, distinctive, and colorful.

- Think of the messages and sayings that you want people to remember about your issue and your group. For example, Leaders Today uses the saying "We are the generation we have been waiting for."

5. Map out actions on a calendar.

- Make sure that you give yourself enough time to plan each action thoroughly.

- Take time for some fun.

- Evaluate your actions regularly.

- How often can the team meet? Where?

6. Media and education.

- How will you create greater awareness of the issue?

- How will you use the media to help?

- How will you advertise what you are doing?

7. Create a budget.

- How much money will you need to carry out your plan? You might need to pay for postage or buy supplies. What else will you need?

- How can money be raised?

- How will transportation be arranged?

- Which companies, organizations, or groups can be approached for donations?

Step 6: Take Action and Then Review

Taking action is key to turning your ideas into reality. If you are planning a Human Rights Awareness Day, make certain you follow through on your idea. If you are collecting school and health kits for children in developing countries, do your very best to collect as many kits as you can. It is actions that create real and lasting change in the world.

Once you have acted, it is important to review and evaluate each action so that you can become more effective. You may want to look at the planning, the actions taken, the media, the people involved, and the results. Here are some questions you may want to ask yourself:

✔ What were the positive aspects of the project?

✔ What were the negative aspects of the project?

✔ How can we improve our project or actions next time?

✔ How well did we work as a team?

✔ What new areas of responsibility do we need to add to our team next time?

✔ How can we be more effective as a team next time?

✔ Did the team members encounter any major obstacles?

✔ What did the team do well to overcome these obstacles?

✔ Were there any major disagreements? If so, did the team work well to settle the disagreements? If not, what steps need to be taken in the future to solve conflicts?

✔ Did the team have enough volunteers, money, equipment, and resources? If not, what can the team do next time to meet our project needs?

✔ Did the team have enough or too much adult guidance and support?

✔ What did each of us learn or gain from this project?

✔ What might each of us do differently next time?

Tip

Write down your answers to the questions and keep them in a file so that they can be reviewed when you start the next project. Although you may find it difficult to criticize your work, constructive criticism can be very valuable. Be proud of your achievements. Enjoy one another's company and try to think of ways to do even better next time.

> There is one thing stronger than all the armies in the world, and that is an idea whose time has come.
>
> — Victor Hugo (1802–1885) Author

Step 7: Have Fun!

Stay motivated. At times, you may feel overwhelmed and may even run into some opposition. When this happens, try to remember why you got involved in the first place. Your goal is to help others make a difference.

Once you have finished your campaign or event, throw a pizza party or go to a movie with your team. Also, do not be afraid of having fun while you are organizing your activities. Try not to lose focus on the task at hand, but do not forget to make your social involvement an enjoyable and memorable experience.

As teammates, inspire and encourage one another. Everyone needs the support and friendship of those who share the same vision and goals. Friends are one of the gifts you give yourself when you get involved in a cause.

Some Thoughts to Keep You Going

- Look at a problem as an opportunity to be creative. Experiment with new ways of addressing the problem. Try the untried.

- Be willing to change, to rotate responsibility, and to find other solutions. Seize every opportunity to learn.

- Look at the big picture. Do not let small obstacles or problems get you down.

- Do not forget the purpose of what you are doing. Your belief in the cause will keep you motivated.

- Work with friends. Seek their support. We all need other people.

- Be optimistic. Focus on the good in others, the good in yourself, and the good you are doing, whether your successes are large or small.

PART 2
The How-To Guide

How to Use the Telephone

Most of you are probably experts when it comes to everyday use of the telephone. You already know that the phone is a great way to get in touch with friends and family, or even to order take-out food. But what you may not know is that the phone can also be a valuable tool for social action. You can use the phone to organize a meeting or event, interview people, conduct opinion polls, or talk to government officials about your concerns. Here are a few ways to make your phone call a success:

Prepare for your call

1. Get permission to use phones at your home or school. Never make long-distance calls without asking.

2. Be organized. Sometimes calling important officials can make you nervous. Before you pick up the phone, prepare a call sheet with the following information, and keep it in front of you while you are speaking with your contact. Being prepared will give you confidence.

- the name of your contact
- the reason for your call/what you want to ask
- your address and telephone number to give to your contact at the end of the call

3. Make sure you have enough space on your call sheet (or have extra paper nearby) to record any information your contact gives you.

Make the call

4. Place the call from a quiet location.

5. When someone answers the phone, speak clearly and tell the person your name and school or organization.

6. If you do not have a contact name, briefly state what kind of information you are looking for and ask to be put in touch with the appropriate individual or department.

7. If your contact is not there, find out when she or he will be available and make yourself a note to call back at that time. You can also leave your name and contact information, a time when you can be reached, and the reason for your call.

8. Do not give up if your contact does not call back right away. Keep calling until you get the information you need, but always remain calm and polite.

When you reach your contact

9. When you do speak with your contact, tell him or her your name and your school or organization, and then explain why you have called.

10. Write down your contact's response. If you miss something, do not be afraid to ask for clarification.

11. Get the correct name, title, address, and phone extension of your contact, and make sure he or she knows how to get in touch with you, too.

When spelling your name, use a word to clarify every letter; for example, "'L' as in lemon, 'A' as in apple," and so on.

12. After the phone call, review your notes and add anything else that you can remember from the conversation.

Finding phone numbers

Phone books are useful tools for locating individuals, organizations, businesses, and government institutions. Most directories have three sections: white, yellow, and blue. The Yellow Pages™ sometimes appear as part of the directory and sometimes as a separate publication.

The **white pages** list, in alphabetical order, the phone number(s) of people as well as companies and organizations. To find a number in the white pages, look up the last name of the person or the first name of the company or organization.

The **Yellow Pages**™ list, in alphabetical order by product or service category, the phone number(s) of businesses, organizations, and professionals. For example, look up *computers* and you will find companies that sell computers; look up *physicians* and you will find a list of medical professionals, arranged alphabetically by last name and sometimes listing their specialty.

Tip

There are many Web sites that provide online phone books. Search the Web to find one that has a listing for your area. This should be a free service.

You can also dial 411 and have the operator do the search for you, but you must know the location and the full name of the person or organization you are calling. There is a fee associated with this service.

The **blue pages** contain government phone numbers. Federal, state, county, and municipal governments each have their own section. To use the blue pages, you must first know which level of government you need. For example, if you are focusing on garbage pick-up, you must speak to someone in the local government. If you want to speak with one of your national elected officials, you must look in the national or federal government section.

Setting up a calling tree

An easy way to let many people know about meetings, actions, and planned events is by setting up a calling tree (an example follows). Be sure to give each caller a complete list of all people on the calling tree. That way, if one caller needs help, another can assist without difficulty. Review and update your list regularly. If any caller proves to be unreliable, substitute her or his name for another.

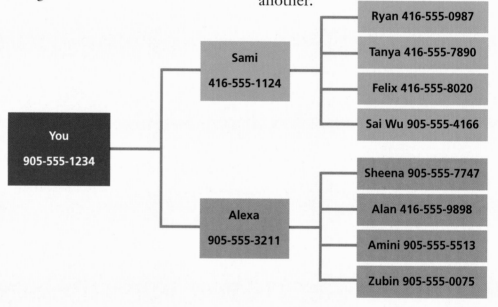

How to Set Up a Group

The first thing to learn about social action is that you cannot take on the world by yourself. No matter how much easier it may sometimes seem to do everything on your own, if you share the work, you will be sure to accomplish more. You will also be giving others the opportunity to get involved in social issues and to realize their potential to be leaders and activists.

The most important skill you will need for the future is teamwork. You will move faster toward your goal if you have the help and support of people who are as dedicated to your cause as you are.

Tip

If people tell you they are interested in helping, keep all their names, email addresses, and phone numbers on a list so you can contact them to make sure they know about meetings.

Building Your Core Group

Step 1: Look for teammates

✔ Who else is committed to solving this problem?

✔ Where can you find them?

✔ What kind of work needs to be done?

✔ What specific skills might others have to offer?

Step 2: Network

To gather a core group of people dedicated to your cause, start with your friends and classmates. You might want to start by making a presentation to your class (see the section Public Speaking beginning on page 37), or by talking to people individually. Or, you might simply put up posters in your school to announce the first meeting. (Inform your teacher or principal of your intention first.) Tell them about the issue you are concerned with, and ask them if they would like to help you take action. Ask people you know if they know of others who would like to get involved and if they can introduce you to them.

The keys to gathering support for your cause are networking and perseverance. Do not give up if some people turn you down at first. You will find that many others will be pleased you asked for their help. Some people do not realize that they have wonderful things to offer a group until you let them know that they are needed.

When recruiting, all existing team members should work to make new members feel welcome. Introduce everyone and inform new members of what the group has been doing.

Step 3: Build on your differences

If you think that everyone in your group has to be the same in order to work well together, think again. An effective group needs a variety of ingredients. When building your team, bring together people with different strengths, talents, perspectives, and experiences. Each person can make a valuable contribution and can help shed new light

Tip

The key to building a strong group is inclusion. Do not leave anyone out just because he or she is different. Celebrating your differences will make you powerful. Your opposition will be impressed when they see all kinds of people supporting the same cause.

The Ingredients for a Great Group

People who are... →	can...
creative	think up clever fundraisers
organized	plan events and keep the group focused
artistic	create posters and information displays
good writers	help group members write speeches or letters
logical	problem-solve
good communicators	network
good at math	take care of finances
enthusiastic	motivate the group

> "The stronger you are as a team, the more power you will have to make a difference!"
>
> — Craig Kielburger (b. 1982) Founder, Kids Can Free the Children

on old perspectives. It is also a good idea to have some younger and some older members in your group. This ensures the group will continue on year after year even though members change.

Bringing out the best in your group

- Find out what skills each person has, and how he or she would be most interested in helping.
- Ask individual members to take the lead in an area where they feel most useful.
- Make sure all members are enthusiastic about the role they will play.
- Create a list of rules concerning conduct that you all agree upon. These rules might

include respecting each member's opinion and acknowledging everyone's right to speak. You might also decide that no one other than the moderator has the right to interrupt others when speaking.

- Use kind words with one another. You are all part of the same team.
- Share and celebrate small victories.

Step 4: Keep building

Reach out to new participants even after your core group is established. Their fresh ideas and new perspectives will revitalize your projects and remind you of why you got involved in the first place. Expand your group by making a list of volunteers who may not be able to dedicate themselves completely to your cause, but who would like to help out when they have time. Ask your volunteers what their special strengths are and how they would be interested in contributing.

Working in groups can be challenging, but the rewards can be great. Remember the TEAM acronym — Together Everyone Achieves More. By working as a team, you will make new friends and will be able to encourage and support one another. You will also be able to accomplish a great deal more.

How to Hold a Meeting

Holding a meeting and providing an opportunity for your team members to share their opinions and ideas can be a powerful force for progress and change. When creative, energetic, and resourceful people come together, anything is possible. However, facilitating an effective meeting can often be tough. It is the leader's job to ensure the opinions of everyone are heard and respected. But he or she must also make certain that the meeting remains productive and on track. The following section will give you some helpful hints on how to hold a successful meeting.

Step 1: Call a Group Meeting

Arrange a date, time, and location for your first meeting. Once you have a list of people who want to be involved, tell them about the meeting. You may want to hold a meeting at your home, at school, or at a community center. Here are some other details you should address:

✔ Select a location that is convenient, accessible, and large enough to accommodate your group. If necessary, obtain permission from an adult, teacher, or parent/guardian to host your meeting at the location you have selected.

✔ Set a convenient time for the meeting.

✔ Remind people about the meeting the day before it is held.

Step 2: Hold a First Meeting

Your first meeting should be simple and short, and viewed as an opportunity for group members to get to know one another. Here are some suggestions for conducting an effective first meeting:

✔ Thank everyone for coming.

✔ Take turns making simple introductions or, if possible, find a quick and fun way to "break the ice" so people feel relaxed and welcomed. If there are people in the room who do not yet know one another, this step is particularly important.

✔ Briefly discuss the issue. Address such questions as: Why are we having this meeting? What are we trying to achieve? How can everyone become involved?

Tip

The best way to attract people to your meetings is to speak to them in person and invite them to come. People are much more likely to attend a meeting if they have been personally asked or if they have been given a distinctive role to play.

Step 3: Hold a Second Meeting

This meeting is key because it often serves as the basis for your organization or group. Make sure everyone gets involved and participates, and try to accomplish some of the following goals:

✔ Educate group members about the issue and encourage them to continuously educate themselves on the topic.

✔ Choose a name for your organization.

✔ Assign a person to design a number of possible logos and develop potential slogans for your group.

✔ Brainstorm what type of action your group will take to effect positive change in your chosen social issue. (See Step 5: Make a Plan of Action beginning on page 11 in Part 1 for some helpful suggestions.)

✔ Set goals and a timeline that will help you achieve the actions that you plan to take in working on your social issue of choice.

✔ Value everyone's input and encourage questions. Make sure that everyone has a chance to speak.

✔ Set a firm date, time, and location for the second meeting, during which many important decisions will be made.

How to Hold Great Meetings

- Always have an agenda for your meeting.

- Try to attract people who show a real interest in your cause.

- Hold your meetings on regular dates and times; for example, every Friday at 3:00 p.m. in Room 212.

- Set goals for each meeting and achieve them. You may want to ask: Why are we having this meeting and what do we want to accomplish?

- Always keep your team members updated. You can achieve this by phone if your group is small, or by email if your group is larger. You may also want to use a bulletin board at school or at your community center.

✔ Consider assigning responsibilities instead of titles.
Some possible roles include the following:

- organizer of the meeting

- organizer of events

- organizer of publicity

- head of recruitment for new members

- group recorder (the person in charge of taking notes at meetings)

- administrator of finances

Create an agenda

An agenda simply outlines the issues that need to be discussed and decided upon by the group. An agenda helps to ensure that everyone stays focused during your meeting and that everything up for discussion is covered before the meeting is over. Here is a sample agenda of a meeting:

Sample Agenda

**Agenda for Teens Taking Action Meeting
— October 21, 20--**

Location: Meeting to be held in Room 212 at 3:45 p.m.

3:45: Meeting to be called to order. Issues to be discussed are as follows:

- Introductions. Welcoming of new members to the group.
- Review of decisions made at the last meeting on October 14.
- Announcements and updates since last meeting.
- Planning the next fundraiser for the group. Teens Taking Action needs to decide
    - what type of fundraiser it will be
    - the date
    - who will be in charge
    - the next steps which will ensure the fundraiser is a success (making a plan of action)
- Discussion of new business.
- Confirmation of the date and time of next meeting.
- Adjournment of meeting.
- Pizza dinner at Zack's Pizzeria for those who are interested.

During the meeting

✔ Start on time.

✔ Follow your agenda.

✔ Make certain the meeting has a leader. Meeting leaders are often referred to as *moderators*. It is the moderator's responsibility to ensure group members participate, are allowed the opportunity to express themselves, and speak in turn. Ideally, take turns assuming the role of moderator so that everyone on the team can learn how to lead meetings.

✔ Supply materials necessary for the meeting, such as pens, paper, display boards, and so on.

✔ Arrange seating for the meeting that will promote discussion (for example, sit in a circle).

✔ Encourage participation.

✔ Avoid getting into too much detail. Less significant items can be addressed at separate meetings.

✔ Try to stay on topic. The moderator can make suggestions to keep the group focused.

✔ As a group, set tasks for people to do for the next meeting.

After the meeting

✔ Call or email members who missed the meeting to update them on what they missed.

✔ Call or email first-time participants and thank them for coming.

✔ Remind people in advance of tasks they agreed to complete before the next meeting.

✔ Distribute to all group members a copy of the notes, also called *minutes*, taken during the meeting so that everyone knows what was discussed and decided upon. Alternatively, email the notes to group members.

How to Make Decisions

Making decisions can be one of the most difficult things your group does. Here are some hints to help you make good decisions:

• Try to decide on a method of decision-making that everyone agrees with. This step may be challenging, but it is necessary. Some groups like to make decisions by majority vote (when a vote is taken by the members of your organization and the position that is most supported is the decision that is followed); others by general agreement, or consensus.

• Consensus is often the best method of decision-making. It encourages people to work to find solutions and guarantees everyone's opinion is respected.

• If you choose to make decisions by majority vote, determine in advance who among the group is eligible to vote. Is it members of the organization or simply people who attend the meetings? Establishing voting eligibility requirements before a disagreement occurs is preferable. Count everyone's vote equally; no one vote should be worth more than any other.

- There may be times when team members either have difficulty making up their mind about an issue, or simply disagree. If this occurs, have the moderator list the pros and cons on a chalkboard or piece of chart paper so that everyone can review both sides of the issue and a clear decision can be made.

- Encourage your moderator to consult various books on running a successful meeting. A librarian will be able to help him or her locate suitable resources.

Writing Letters

Writing letters is a good way to tell people what you think, to ask for information, or to work with people in government or organizations. This section will help you write effective letters. You will find helpful examples of several letters written by young people, including:

- letter to request information
- thank-you letter
- letter to a politician
- letter to the editor of a newspaper or magazine

When writing any letter, keep the following hints in mind:

- ✔ Type or write your letter neatly. It may look better if it is double-spaced.

- ✔ Include the date, your complete return address, phone number, and email address (if applicable) so that you can be contacted.

- ✔ Have someone reliable check your letter for spelling mistakes and grammatical errors.

Tip

If the organization from which you are requesting information says that there is a cost for the materials, tell them that you are a student, briefly explain your group's mandate, and then ask if they would be willing to donate the materials or provide them at a reduced cost.

Letter to Request Information

Writing a letter to request information is an easy way to gather materials for your research. Many organizations have information kits for that purpose. When writing a letter to request information, follow these guidelines:

✔ Try to follow the layout in the sample letter as closely as possible. It is a style of letter that is considered professional and is used often in business circles.

✔ Be as specific as possible in your request, especially when you are asking for government information. Governments have thousands of publications on hundreds of issues. If you are precise and clear when you describe what type of information you need, you are more likely to get the most useful information possible.

✔ Ask the organization to send you an information package for young people, if they have one.

Format of a Letter Requesting Information

Your name
Your full address
Your telephone, fax, and email information

Date the letter

Name of organization
Person to whom you are writing
Full address

Dear (Mr., Mrs., or Ms. and last name)

• Identify yourself (state your name, grade, and school).
• Briefly describe your group.
• State your purpose for writing.
• Thank the person to whom you are writing for his or her time.
• Let the person know that you look forward to hearing from him or her.

Sincerely,

Sign your name

Type or print your name

Sample Letter Requesting Information

Ari Khan
14th Avenue East
Seattle, WA 23456
Tel: 206-555-0202
Fax: 206-555-1314

October 21, 20—

Children for the Environment
16 Balsam Road
Boulder, CO 34567

Dear Children for the Environment:

My name is Ari Khan. I am a ninth-grade student at Willfolk Public High School in Seattle. My classmates and I have started a group called Youth Heroes. We are concerned about loss of habitat for animals across the United States.

I am writing to request an information package on loss of animal habitat in the United States, and want to know how our group can help. If you have a package designed specifically for youth, this would be very helpful, as most of our members are between the ages of 10 and 15.

Thank you for your time. I look forward to hearing from you.

Sincerely,

Ari Khan

Ari Khan

Thank-You Letter

It is important to thank the people who help you. Often, groups lose support simply because they forget to acknowledge the assistance of others. Thanking your supporters will make them more open to helping you again in the future, if necessary. When writing this type of letter, follow these guidelines:

✔ Be sincere and make the letter personal.

✔ Refer to the gift or service that was donated.

✔ Tell the donor how she or he helped your group and the cause.

✔ Express your gratitude and keep in touch with this individual.

> No person can become rich without himself enriching others.
>
> — **Andrew Carnegie (1835–1919) Industrialist and philanthropist**

Sample Thank-You Letter

Anitra Jacobs
Belleview High School
17 Maple Drive
Smithtown, NY 12345

May 13, 20—

Mr. James Chan
T-Shirts R Us
132 Wallace Street
Smithtown, NY 12345

Dear Mr. Chan,

On behalf of the students at Belleview High School, I would like to thank you for your generous donation of 50 T-shirts for our rock-a-thon fundraiser.

We had more than 500 people attend the event and raised $1200, which will go toward building a school for needy children in Calcutta. These funds will help provide these children with an education and the opportunity to break free from the cycle of poverty.

We thank you again for your help. We will keep you informed about our work.

Gratefully,

Anitra Jacobs

Anitra Jacobs

Contacting Public Officials

Politicians are elected by adults, but it is their job to represent all people in the area in which they were elected (their constituency), including you. They also make and change laws, so they are good people to contact if you want to make a difference.

In the United States, there are four basic levels of government: federal, state, county, and municipal (towns, villages, and cities). Each level of government has specific responsibilities, some of which are outlined below. Note that many of these responsibilities overlap between the different levels.

Municipal

Municipal governments are in charge of villages, towns, and cities and usually comprise the following individuals:

- mayor or city manager
- councilors, selectmen, supervisors, or commissioners (local politicians who help run the village, town, or city)
- school board trustees (representatives on educational matters)

County

County governments are in charge of counties (subdivisions of states). A county government usually consists of the following individuals:

- mayor or county executive
- councilors, supervisors, or commissioners (local politicians who help run the county)

State

State governments are in charge of the states. A state government consists of the following individuals:

- governor
- attorney general (the head of the state's legal department)
- senators, representatives, delegates, or assemblymen

Federal

The federal government is in charge of the country. It is split up into three branches, the executive branch, the legislative branch, and the judicial branch, which are organized to balance each other in powers and responsibilities. The federal government consists of the following elected officials (plus many more who are appointed by the government):

- president
- vice president
- senators
- representatives

When contacting government officials, keep in mind that certain powers are reserved for the federal government and other powers have been given to state, county, or municipal governments.

County Responsibilities

Administering welfare programs

Elections

Public libraries

Maintenance of highways and bridges

Making county laws and setting taxes

Sheriff's department

State Responsibilities

Education

Health

Housing and urban development

Regulations relating to property, industry, business, and public utilities

State police

The state criminal code

Transportation

Working conditions

Welfare

Municipal Responsibilities

By-laws for the municipality

Licensing

Maintenance of roads and public buildings

Parks and recreation

Police department

Public libraries

Waste disposal (garbage collection, sewers, recycling, etc.)

Zoning

Federal Responsibilities

Agriculture

Commerce

Defense

Education

Energy

Environment

Finance

Foreign relations

Health

Housing and urban development

Justice

Labor

Military

Transportation

You can also write to politicians and leaders of any other country in the world. To obtain an address and name of a foreign head of state, simply contact the embassy of that country. Ask how the head of state should be addressed in a letter (for example, "Your Majesty…" or "Dear President…"). Also ask for the proper spelling of the person's name.

Writing Letters to Government Officials

When writing a letter to a head of state, politician, or public official, try to keep in mind the following:

✔ Address the official using his or her correct title.

✔ Stick to one issue per letter.

✔ Do your homework — make sure you accurately describe the problem or issue, and double-check any facts or statistics you use.

✔ Speak from your own experience or knowledge.

✔ Ask the official for her or his views on the situation.

✔ If you disagree with the point of view of the public official, do so in a polite and respectful manner.

Format for a Letter to a Public Official

> Your name
> Your full address
> Telephone, fax, and email information
>
> Date the letter

Name of public official
Full address

Dear (name of public official or other title),

- Identify yourself: State your full name, grade, and school.

- State your purpose in writing: Explain why you are writing. If it is about a specific bill or law, make reference to it or state its name or number.

- Express your feelings: Tell the politician what you think about the issue. Explain why the cause is important to you.

State any solutions you or your group have for the problem.

- Explain what you want:
  Tell the official why you are writing. You may want the individual to support or oppose a certain bill or law. You may want him or her to create a law regarding an issue.

- Say "thank you":
  Remember to thank the official and state that you look forward to hearing from him or her.

> Sincerely,
>
> Type or print your name and sign in the space above

Sample Letter to a Public Official

Eric LeBlanc
121 Sparrow Way
Jamestown, ND 45678

December 6, 20—

President George W. Bush
The White House
1600 Pennsylvania Avenue NW
Washington, D.C. 20500

Dear Mr. President,

My name is Eric LeBlanc and I am in the eighth grade at Meadowvale School in Jamestown, North Dakota. I am writing to you about the issue of child labor and the exploitation of children in developing countries. I have done a lot of research on the subject and have discovered that there are over 250 million child laborers in the world who work for pennies a day.

I believe that child labor is wrong and should be stopped. I am aware that you visit many countries and discuss international trade. I believe that this is a good thing, but please do not forget about the children who are working in hazardous conditions when you sign trade deals. I am a young person also and I believe that these children deserve a better chance.

One way to help these children is by supporting the Rugmark label. It is a label indicating that a particular carpet was not made from the exploitation of children.

I look forward to hearing from you. Thank you for your time and consideration.

Sincerely,

Eric LeBlanc

Eric LeBlanc

Some titles you may need to know:

- For the president of the United States, address your letter to "President (then include the full name)," and use the greeting "Dear Mr. (or Madam) President."

- For a former president of the United States, address your letter to "The Honorable (then include the full name)," and use the greeting "Dear Mr. (or Mrs. or Ms.) (then the last name)."

- For a U.S. senator, address your letter to "The Honorable (then include the full name)," and use the greeting "Dear Senator (then the last name)."

- For a U.S. representative, address your etter to "The Honorable (then include the full name)," and use the greeting "Dear Mr. (or Mrs. or Ms.) (then the last name)."

- For a governor, address your letter to "The Honorable (then the last name), Governor of (name of state)," and use the greeting "Dear Governor (then the last name)."

- For a mayor, address your letter to "The Honorable (then include the full name); His (or Her) Honor the Mayor," and use the greeting "Dear Mayor (then the last name)."

Letter to the Editor

Most newspapers have an editorial page and it is to this page that readers can write letters about matters that concern them. The newspaper decides which letters to publish according to what it believes will interest the paper's readership. Writing a letter to the editor is a good way to voice your opinion and to educate people in your community about important issues. Many people who read the newspaper read these letters.

The following tips will be useful if you decide to write a letter to the editor:

✔ Editor contact information is usually listed in the editorial section of the newspaper or in the first few pages of a magazine. You can send your letter by email, fax, or regular mail.

✔ If you are writing about an article you read in a particular newspaper or magazine, cite the date, title, writer, and subject of the article in your letter. Responding to a recently published article is one of the best ways to increase your chances of your letter being published.

✔ Keep your letter simple. Make it brief and to the point (or it will not be printed). A short letter that does not include unnecessary information is more likely to be read.

✔ Do your homework. Make certain that all your facts are accurate. Do not exaggerate. Your credibility will be put to the test. Anyone can respond to or criticize your comments.

✔ Be polite. Remember that you are representing young people.

✔ Create a headline. Editors are always looking for short and interesting headlines. Make their job easier by writing the headline yourself.

✔ Make it personal. Editors are more likely to publish a letter if you use personal experiences or give personal opinions.

✔ Proofread, proofread, proofread.

✔ If you send your letter by fax or mail, sign your work. Newspapers require a signature, which legally allows them to print the letter. They may phone you to ensure that you wrote the letter yourself, so include your phone number.

✔ Do not be discouraged if your letter is not published. Keep trying!

Format for a Letter to the Editor

Your name
Your full address
Telephone, fax, and email information

Date the letter

Editor of (newspaper)
Full address and fax number

- Identify yourself:
  State your full name, your grade, and school.
- State the purpose of your letter:
  If you are writing in response to an article, mention the date, title, and subject. Briefly explain your cause and state what you are trying to do to help.
- Express your feelings:
  Express your likes or dislikes about the article you have read. Tell the editor why the cause is important to you. Mention any solutions to the problem.
- Say "thank you":
  Always thank the editor for her or his time.

Sincerely,

Type or print your name and
sign in the space above.

Sample Letter to the Editor

Sara Crane
1123 Main Street
Mansfield, OH 56789

February 4, 20—

Mansfield Times
44 Nelson Street
Mansfield, OH 56789

To the Editor:

My name is Sara Crane. I am in the ninth grade at Mansfield Prep in Mansfield. I am writing in response to the article "Recycling Stops," which was in your paper on January 18. I am very concerned about the environment and have started a group called Enviro Kids.

I am upset because the article says that the picking up of blue boxes will stop in my area next year due to government cutbacks. This is terrible and means that more waste will end up in huge garbage dumps. Young people will be inheriting this earth. I believe that we all have a serious responsibility to protect our environment. I believe that the recycling program should be saved and that more programs should be created throughout the county. If we only invested as much money in our environment as we do in industries that cause pollution, we would all benefit.

Thank you for your time and consideration.

Sincerely,

Sara Crane
Sara Crane

> "Do not go where the path may lead, go instead where there is no path and leave a trail.
>
> — **Ralph Waldo Emerson (1803–1882) Lecturer, poet, and essayist**

Writing a letter to the editor can be a lot of hard work, but it is very exciting when you see your letter in print. Vanessa Nicholas was upset about a national campaign in Canada in which children were asked to make a choice among their basic human rights. She decided to take action. She wrote a letter to the editor of *The Toronto Star*, which was published and seen by millions of people. The text of her letter follows.

Letter to the Editor by Vanessa Nicholas

All rights for all children

As a Grade 12 student, I was appalled when I heard about the Nov. 19 election being held by UNICEF Canada and Elections Canada on the rights of a child.

(The vote is being held to mark the 10th anniversary of Canada's endorsement of the United Nations Convention on the Rights of the Child.)

Why should children from across Canada choose from 10 fundamental, pre-chosen rights when we are entitled to all 54 articles outlined by the 1989 U.N. Convention?

These rights cannot be separated because they are completely inter-connected; one means nothing without the others.

Although the organizers might have had good intentions, they failed to look at all sides of their plan. We children know when we are being given crumbs.

Why are we not being asked to vote on something substantial, such as electing a children's commissioner?

This vote will not have a positive effect; it sends a message that one right is more important than the others. Here are two examples:

- Sue is a very happy 8-year-old. She loves school. She loves her family and she loves to play. Now her teachers, the people she trusts, are asking her to choose which is most important to her. How can she choose between having a family, her parents, and little brother Mikey, and going to school?

- Bob is a homeless boy. How can he choose between the right to protection from harm and the right to food and shelter? Unfortunately, Bob will not even be given a chance to vote.

Not all of Canada's children are being given a chance to vote. There will be no polling stations set up for children who do not attend school.

This vote goes against my own morals and values.

How can I choose between my education, protection from harm, or my family, whom I love very much?

I think we all have to ask ourselves a vital question: Is this vote in the best interests of children or is it to make the adults look good?

On Nov. 19, we, the children of Canada, should not choose from among our rights — we should choose for them.

We can send a loud and clear message by writing across our ballots: "All rights for all children."

Vanessa Nicholas
Mississauga

Public Speaking

Speaking is one of the most exciting ways to deliver your message. It can spark enthusiasm, interest, and action from those who hear you. People sometimes feel nervous or afraid to speak in front of groups. What these individuals do not realize, however, is that public speaking is easier when you take the time to practice. It can also be lots of fun.

How to Write a Speech

Writing your speech can be the best part of your public-speaking experience. Putting your ideas on paper gives you the chance to completely think through your ideas before you are in front of an audience.

Before you begin writing, however, make certain that you have done your homework. Search the Internet and libraries, interview people, and think of stories from your own experience. For research hints, see Step 2: Do Your Research in Part 1, beginning on page 4.

What follows is a list of the three essential components of every speech.

Part 1: Introduction

- If you have not been introduced by someone, state your name, grade, and school.

- If you have been introduced, you may want to begin with an interesting quote or a shocking statistic to grab the audience's attention.

- State what you will speak about (your main points), why you became involved in your issue, and why it is important to you.

Part 2: Body of the Speech

- Make it interesting and creative. Provide any facts or statistics that you obtained through researching your subject.

- Share with the audience real-world examples of people affected by the issue.
- Tell a story. You might focus on something that happened to you while working on your issue, or on something that you read about while doing your research.
- Explain what you are trying to accomplish and what the future holds for your cause.

Part 3: Conclusion

- End the speech by summarizing your main points. The conclusion should be a short statement — a message the audience will remember.
- Briefly explain how audience members can become involved in your campaign. (Ask for action on their part.)
- Inform listeners that you will stay to answer questions after your speech. You may want to bring some flyers to hand out.
- Thank the audience for their time and attention.

The Do's and Don'ts of Delivering a Speech

One of the secrets to giving a great speech is to enjoy speaking about the social issue that inspires you. Here are a few tips:

Do's

- Wait for the noise in the room to die down before you begin.
- Make eye contact; look at your audience and smile.
- Direct your speech to the entire audience, not just to those people immediately in front of you or on one side of the room.
- Wear comfortable clothes that are appropriate for the presentation.
- Speak slowly, loudly, and clearly.

Don'ts

- Don't clasp your hands, hold them behind your back, or put them in your pockets. Hold a pen in your hand, if necessary.
- Don't exaggerate your hand movements.
- Don't move your feet or shift your weight from one leg to the other too often. Doing so can distract the audience.
- Don't chew gum.
- Don't read your speech. Some speakers memorize their entire speech, while others periodically refer to speaking notes written on index cards, which is acceptable.

Stories are sometimes the best way to convey an idea to an audience. You might tell the audience how you first became socially involved. Or, perhaps you could recount the story of a young person you have met who has been negatively affected by the problem or social issue you are trying to change. Try to be descriptive, using words that draw pictures in the minds of your listeners.

Posture is another important element in public speaking. Your presentation must not only sound good, it must also look good. Often, your delivery is just as important as what you are saying. Standing correctly, smiling, and appearing relaxed (even if you are nervous) are key components of a successful speech.

Energy can be contagious. If you are energetic and full of enthusiasm about your subject, you just might spark that same passion in your listeners. If you are speaking to fellow students or to a younger audience, you may have to heighten the intensity of your presentation in order to hold their attention.

Ask for action. This is something that many speakers forget to do. If you are speaking about an important social issue, tell your listeners how they, too, can become active in your campaign. Offer them three avenues to involvement: (1) A simple action, like signing a petition at the back of the room; (2) A more difficult action, such as donating $10 to your cause; (3) A significant action, such as learning more about the issue and telling people at their school, work, or place of worship about the problem.

Know your audience. To whom will you be speaking? You do not want to give the same speech to students in Grade 5 that you would to a Senate committee. Try to adapt your speech to your audience.

Interesting facts and statistics add credibility to what you are saying and help to convey the importance of your issue. Did you know that half the people in this world have never made a telephone call? It's true! Remember, never make up facts or statistics; obtain them from reliable sources.

No reading! Reading shows the audience that you are not prepared to give your speech. Having notes or cue cards listing major points is fine, but the most powerful presentations are delivered from the heart. Make certain, however, that you take the time to familiarize yourself with the main ideas in your speech. Then practice, practice, practice.

Give from the heart. This is the most important thing to remember when you speak. Why are you passionate about your issue? Who are the people you are trying to help? Believe in yourself and in your ability to make a difference.

Smile.

Chin up.

You may want to hold a pen if you tend to put your hands in your pockets.

Keep your shoulders relaxed.

Do not move your hips too much.

Keep your feet secure on the ground and do not "dance."

You may want to stand with one foot slightly forward.

 Tip

Tips for Memorizing
- Read your speech over and over again. Read it silently. Read it out loud. Read it to your family, friends, or even your pet.
- Record your speech on tape and listen to it when you have some free time: on your way to school, before bed, or while brushing your teeth.
- Write out your speech several times. Eventually, you will no longer need your notes.
- Have someone videotape you giving your speech and play it back so that you can see what the audience will see.

Sample Speech

Ladies and Gentlemen,

(INTRODUCTION)

My name is Catherine Wong. I am 13 years old and in the eighth grade at Parkview Middle School. I am a member of the group Kids Helping the Homeless. We are a group of young people working to help the less fortunate in our community. Did you know that our homeless population has grown by more than 4% every year for the past five years? Did you know that 40% of the people who are out on the streets are under 20 years of age, many coming from broken and abusive homes? In my opinion, however, the saddest fact is that the programs that are supposed to help the homeless are about to have their funding cut by the City Council. We do not think that this is fair!

(BODY and STORY)

Homeless people are just like you and me. Last night, when you and I were tucked into our warm beds, they slept on the cold, hard pavement of our city streets. When our school went to visit the local food bank, we met homeless people in line for baskets of food, and realized just how lucky we were. One woman I met, named Sandra, had been living on the streets for the past two years. She had a dog named Benny who was very cute and friendly. She told me that because she had her dog, which she kept for company, she was not allowed into the shelters. Sandra ended up on the streets because she was abused at home. Out on her own, she could not find work. She was really a nice person, funny and interesting.

I felt really sad knowing that she and Benny would not have a home to go to that night. I did some research and found out that there are not enough homeless shelters to accommodate the number of people currently on the streets. I also found out that two homeless people died on the streets of our city last year because of the cold. I don't think that this is fair, do you?

Our group, Kids Helping the Homeless, is trying to make a difference. We are helping our community by collecting old coats, blankets, and sleeping bags to give to shelters. We are also making food baskets so that homeless people can eat a nourishing meal. As well, we are asking the City Council to pass a bill that will give more money to the construction of shelters for the homeless.

(CONCLUSION)

Today, however, we are asking for your help. You can do one of three things: (1) Sign our petition at the back of the room, asking the City Council to pass a bill regarding the homeless; (2) Call or write your elected officials at the national level and tell them you think the homeless problem should be an urgent issue on the national agenda; (3) Donate $20 to help make a "cold kit" to give to homeless people during the winter months. But, most importantly, please be nice to homeless people.

If you would like more information or are interested in getting involved in our campaign, please let me know. I would be happy to answer any questions. Thank you for your time.

How to Do a Survey

Sometimes you need to know what people think about an issue or an idea. For example, you might want to find out how many people would attend a particular event before you go to the trouble of organizing it. Or, you might want to know how many people are affected by a certain problem in your community and how they feel about the solution your team has come up with.

A survey is an excellent tool for

✔ determining public opinion

✔ gathering information

✔ raising awareness about an issue

Surveys can also help you to identify opposition to your cause or, alternatively, help you gather support for it. You might find people who agree with your solutions to a social problem and are interested in joining your team. Conducting a survey can change your perspective about an issue, and help you to develop a broader and more informed point of view.

Four Steps to a Successful Survey

Step 1: Do your homework

- Surveys require a lot of work and co-operation from others, so you should only consider conducting a survey if you have a clear purpose in mind. Do you feel that you need specific information from your classmates or community members in order to effectively tackle your social issue? Is there any other way — for example, through research — that you could obtain the type of information you need before you begin? Even if you do decide that a survey is necessary, it is important to conduct some preliminary research before you begin.

- Think about the people who will be answering your questions. Do you want to survey a specific group, or can your questions be answered by anyone?

Step 2: Write a questionnaire

- Each person who responds to your survey needs a separate questionnaire on which to record the answers.

- Write the title of the survey at the top of the questionnaire.

- Provide the name and address of your group so people can return their questionnaire. Thank them for their time.

- Indicate the purpose of your survey.

- State what you intend to do with the results.

- Choose the format for your questions: short answer, check-off lists, *yes* or *no* questions, statements requiring a degree of assent (for example, *strongly agree*, *agree*, *disagree*, *strongly disagree*). It is best to include a variety of questions in your survey, as well as instructions for how to answer them.

- Leave space for answers to be filled in.

- Try to avoid questions that require long answers as they discourage people from responding and can be difficult to interpret.

- Limit the number of questions in your survey. Only ask questions that are important to your research. If the survey can be filled out quickly, more people will be inclined to respond.

Step 3: Conduct your survey

- Surveys can be done in person, by phone, or by mail. Some people dislike being called at home, and some will be reluctant to respond to your letters. So, the best way to do a survey is the direct way: in person. When you can tell people face-to-face how much you appreciate their opinion, it will be more difficult for them to walk away.

- You can conduct surveys in public places, such as your school, neighborhood community center, or mall, but you may have to obtain permission in advance. You may need to have a teacher or a parent/guardian with you to supervise. (**Note:** Never go door-to-door without having an adult accompany you.)

Tip

The more people who answer your survey, the more accurate it will be.

- Distribute copies of the questionnaire to as many people as possible.

- Take plenty of copies of your survey and plenty of pens. There is nothing worse than running out of supplies just when you spot a huge group of people coming your way.

- Remember to be friendly and polite. Some people will not be as willing to participate in your survey as others. Keep your cool, thank them anyway, and move on to the next candidate.

- Some people might disagree with the ideas in your survey. Use this opportunity to find out what they would suggest as an alternative.

Step 4: Assess the results

- Once you have received as many questionnaires as possible, tabulate the results, organize the information using charts and tables, and write a report.

- When analyzing your results, think about how they reflect the group of people who participated in your survey. Did an equal number of males and females answer your questions? Were they of various ages and ethnic backgrounds? Were they from different geographic locations? The answer does not have to be *yes*; just be sure to consider this aspect of your survey when interpreting its results.

- Let other people know what you have discovered through your survey and why it is important. Set up an information booth or use the results of your survey in a flyer or poster. How do people react to your findings? Motivate them to take action and join your team.

Sample Survey

Please answer the following questions by putting a check mark ☑ in the appropriate space. When you are finished, please return this survey to Kim Chong.

Please check one of the following: ❏ Male ❏ Female

Age: ❏ under 10 ❏ 11–15 ❏ 16–18
❏ 19–25 ❏ 26–30 ❏ over 30

1. Have you ever taken action (or helped) on a social issue (environment, poverty, education, etc.)? Check one.
❏ Yes ❏ No

2. If *yes*, in what types of social action did you get involved? Please check all those that apply to you.
❏ School (education) ❏ Human Rights
❏ Environmental ❏ Children's Rights
❏ Community (homelessness, poverty) ❏ Other (please specify) _____

3. Do you belong to an organization working on social or human rights issues?
❏ Yes ❏ No

4. If *yes*, is this organization run by adults or young people?
❏ Adults ❏ Young people

5. Would you like to become involved in an organization working for children's rights?
❏ Yes ❏ No

6. I believe that most young people want to become involved in a social issue. Do you… (check one).
❏ Strongly agree ❏ Agree ❏ Disagree ❏ Strongly disagree ❏ Do not know

7. Why do you think that young people do not become involved in social issues or human rights issues? Check as many as you like.
❏ Do not know an issue ❏ More interested in sports
❏ Cannot find an issue ❏ More interested in television
❏ No adult support ❏ Other (please specify) _____

8. Can you name any organizations dealing with social and human rights that are run by young people between the ages of 10 and 18?

_____   _____

_____   _____

9. We need more groups or organizations dealing with social issues in which youth (ages 10–18) have a voice in decision-making. Check one.
❏ Yes ❏ No

Thank you for taking the time to complete our survey.

How to Write a Petition

If you are concerned about something, and you think other people share your point of view, you can use a petition to gather support for your idea. A petition is a powerful tool for a community. It lets decision-makers know that a lot of people are concerned about a particular issue. It asks them to take action to bring about change.

You can use a petition to effect change at your school, in your community, or at the municipal, county, state, or federal levels of the government.

Format for a Petition

Give it a title

To: **To whom are you giving the petition?**

From: **Identify your group. Are you all from the same school? From the community? From an organization?**

State your purpose: **State the reason for submitting a petition and supply the facts to support your submission.**

Make your request: **The petition must include a request. What do you want the person(s) receiving the petition to do to solve the problem?**

Collect signatures: **Collect as many signatures as you can. Be sure to get a full address beside each name, including city and zip code.**

Present your petition: **Present your petition to a person who will listen to you and who has the power to make changes.**

Sample Petition

Let's Have Lunch Outside

To: Mr. Stedwill, Principal of Hillcrest School
From: Students of Hillcrest School

We, the students of Hillcrest School, would like to be able to eat lunch outside during the spring and the fall. It gets extremely hot inside the classrooms and they are very uncomfortable. It is very difficult to concentrate in class during the afternoon. We would like to eat our lunch outside in the fresh air. We would eat on school grounds and would follow the appropriate rules regarding clean-up.

Name	Grade	Homeroom
_____	_____	_____
_____	_____	_____
_____	_____	_____
_____	_____	_____
_____	_____	_____
_____	_____	_____
_____	_____	_____

How to Write a Petition to the Government

A petition to the government should be written just like any other petition, stating who you are, the purpose of your petition, what you want the government to do about the problem, and your list of signatures. Addresses should also be included for all the signers. Make sure you send your petition to the right level of government (see page 30 for lists of basic responsibilities for the different levels of government). If you want to petition the federal government on a national or international issue, you can send your petition straight to the White House, but it will probably get more attention if you address it to your local congressman or the head of a particular committee or department.

- Print your petition on letter-sized or legal-sized paper.

- The petition should be clear and to the point.

- Always be polite and use appropriate language.

- Do not attach any other documents to the petition, such as maps, pictures, or newspaper articles.

- Collect as many signatures as possible.

- The petitioner's address must be written directly on the petition. The petitioner may give his or her full home address or simply the city and state.

TAKE ACTION!

Format for a Petition to the Government

1. Identify yourself.

We, the undersigned, (identify who the petitioners are)
- citizens or residents of the United States.
- residents of the state of_____
- residents of the city/town of_____
- students from _____ School

2. State your purpose.
Draw your attention to the following:

That,

State the reason why you are submitting a petition and supply facts to support your statement.

3. Make your request.
The petition must have a request. The request should be clear and to the point.

Therefore, your petitioners request that....

State what actions the government should or should not take to solve the problem.

4. Signatures.

Sample Petition to the Congress of the United States

A Petition to the Congress of the United States

Students of Hillcrest Academy,
Milton, Massachusetts.

We, the undersigned, students from Hillcrest Academy, draw the attention of the Congress to the following:

THAT incidents of accidental shootings are becoming more and more frequent, exemplified by the recent shooting at Barclays Public School;
THAT each incident of misuse of guns can hurt the public;
THAT proper legislation can prevent these accidents;
THEREFORE, your petitioners request that Congress support legislation for stronger gun control.

Printed Name	Signature	Address

How to Raise Public Awareness and Support

This section outlines the skills and tools you need to accurately and effectively get your message out to the public. You will learn the following:

- How to make great posters, flyers, and pamphlets.
- How to write an effective press release for newspapers, radio, and television.
- How to make a public service announcement.
- How to give an interview that is so effective it just might make it on the evening news.
- How to create a user-friendly Web site.

How to Use the Media

Every time you pick up a newspaper, watch TV, or turn on the radio, you are being influenced by the media. But the media can be one of the most powerful tools when you are trying to get an important message out to the public. For example, you can spend three weeks giving 10 speeches throughout your community and potentially reach 1,000 people. Or, you may reach the same number of people, if not many more, simply by giving an interview on your local television station. You can use the media to help further your cause.

The word *media* is actually the plural form of the word *medium*, defined as a means through which something else acts. The media are a tool for getting your message across and include the following:

- ✔ posters, flyers, and pamphlets
- ✔ newspapers
- ✔ public service announcements (PSAs)
- ✔ radio
- ✔ television
- ✔ the Internet

The basics

Anytime you send a message to the public, it is a good idea to imagine that you are hearing the message for the very first time. Make certain that you include all important information. For example, telling people about your event will not help you accomplish your goal if you forget to tell them where or when the event is taking place.

> Shoot for the moon. Even if you miss you'll land among the stars.
>
> — **Les Brown (b. 1934) Environmentalist and author**

When you are communicating with the media, be sure to address the five Ws + H:

- Who?
- What?
- When?
- Where?
- Why?
- How?

These are all easy, inexpensive ways of using the media to your advantage. The more care you take in designing them, the more effective they can be.

Using Posters, Flyers, and Pamphlets Effectively

Posters

Making posters is an easy way to advertise, advance your cause, and raise awareness. Here are some techniques for effective poster design:

✔ Make them large, colorful, eye-catching, and easy to read from a distance.

✔ Include the name of your organization and necessary contact information.

✔ Consider including some kind of picture or group logo.

✔ Post them in places where they will have the most exposure to your intended audience.

Flyers

Flyers are simple handouts used to inform people about events. They are designed to reach large numbers of people and can be easily distributed throughout entire communities.

✔ Make one flyer, proofread it, and then, when you are confident it is free of errors, photocopy as many as you need. Consider using recycled paper (even though it sometimes costs a little more). See the section How to Raise Funds beginning on page 66 for tips on how to get copies made free of charge.

- ✔ Copy your flyer on relatively good-quality white or colored paper.

- ✔ Obtain permission to leave stacks of your flyers in stores or at the information desks of libraries and community centers. Hand out flyers at train, subway, or bus station entrances. Get permission to post flyers on bulletin boards at coffee shops or other businesses that have them.

Pamphlets

Distributing pamphlets is a wonderful way to educate people about your group and its mandate. Pamphlets are often made from a standard sheet of paper folded into three panels, with different pieces of information on each panel. You should include the following information in your pamphlet:

- ✔ Background information on your group.

- ✔ Information on the problem you are trying to solve. Consider including two or three key facts or statistics.

- ✔ The projects your group has started or is hoping to support.

- ✔ Information on how others can get involved and help.

- ✔ Contact information for people who wish to get in touch with your group.

Once your pamphlet is designed and printed, the next question you have to think about is how you are going to get it into the hands of the people who will be interested in your cause. Here are some helpful suggestions for the distribution of pamphlets:

- ✔ Leave pamphlets at the community information desk at your local library or community center after you have obtained permission to do so.

- ✔ Request permission to hand out the pamphlets to your peers and friends at your school, place of worship, or at an extracurricular activity.

- ✔ If you give any speeches or presentations to groups, have pamphlets on hand for people who might be interested in more information.

How to Write a Press Release

Are you organizing an important event? Are you planning a big fundraiser for your community, or an information session about your social issue for the entire school? How can you tell the press about what is taking place?

The answer is that you can communicate with the press using a press release. This is one way businesses, charities, and governments inform the press about issues that are important to them. By sending a press release to the local media, you can tell the press about your event and obtain valuable free publicity for your cause if the press profiles what you are doing.

Here are some hints on how to write a press release:

- Follow as closely as possible the sample outlined on the next page.

- Give the press plenty of advanced notice. If a reporter only hears about your event at the last minute, she or he may not have time to attend.

- Fax or email your press release to the reporter three times: (1) One week before your event; (2) 48 hours before your event; and (3) 24 hours before your event. You may want to send it out fewer times to small newspapers, or if you have already heard back from the reporter confirming his or her attendance. You may also want to update your press release if, for example, you have been able to confirm the appearance of a local celebrity at your event, or if other additional information is now available.

- Ensure your press release looks professional. Check your information for accuracy and have someone edit it for spelling and grammar. Finally, double-space your press release so that it is easy to read.

- Keep it short and to the point. Include important information and make it interesting, but avoid including too many details. Doing so might lead the reporter to think she or he can write the story without having to attend your event.

- Write your press release in the third person so that it sounds impartial.

- Include the contact name and phone number of one person in your group. Consider borrowing someone's cell phone for a few days leading up to the event and for the day of the event itself. This will make it easier for reporters to reach you. Make certain, however, that you turn off your phone during class.

- At the end of your press release, include the following symbol: -30-. The press recognizes -30- as a signal that the end of the article has been reached.

Format for a Press Release

PRESS RELEASE

Title of the Press Release (make it sound interesting)

Contact Person's Name
Full Address
Telephone and Fax Numbers
Cell-Phone Number (if you have one)
Email Address

Date of the Press Release

1. State your purpose/describe your event.

   Clearly express the purpose of the press release and what your event involves. The first sentence is the most important. It should be interesting and contain newsworthy information.

2. Identify yourself or your group.

   State who you are (your name, age, school, etc.) and who you represent (the name of your group).

3. Location, times, and dates.

   Describe when and where the event will take place.

4. Other information.

   Include any other important details, such as the confirmed appearance of a local celebrity, or the goal of your event (for example, the amount of money you hope to raise).

5. End Note.

   If the press release is more than one page, write *more* at the bottom of each page. On the last page, write *-30-* at the bottom to indicate that you are finished. This will make you look professional.

Sample Press Release

PRESS RELEASE

KIDS TAKE TO THE STREETS

Judy Steinberg
321 Nelson Street
Georgetown, SC
Tel: 843-555-9890
Fax: 843-555-3434
Kidshelping@hotmail.com

October 25, 20—

On November 3, the youth of Georgetown will be taking to the streets to participate in a 10-mile walkathon to raise funds for cystic fibrosis research.

The event is being organized by the Grade 9 students of South Ridge High in Georgetown. The students of the school have started a group called Kids Helping Kids and are trying to reach a goal of $5000 to donate to cystic fibrosis research.

The walkathon will start at 9:00 a.m. on Saturday, November 3, in front of the town library. William Lawson, local social activist, as well as a player for the Carolina Panthers football team, will be speaking at the opening ceremonies.

Pledge forms are available at all local libraries or by downloading one from our Web site. Spectators are most welcome. It is estimated that over 1,000 young people will participate and "take to the streets."

–30–

Here are some hints for contacting the press:

- Carefully pick the event that you want the press to cover because they will probably only cover one or two of your events per year.

- Most press people are not interested, for example, in simply covering a car wash for charity. Make certain that the event you want covered is important and newsworthy enough to attract the press. Or, you can make your car wash more interesting to the press by, perhaps, inviting and confirming the attendance of the mayor and other city councilors, and adding the promise of a water fight at the end of the day (with the consent of the invitees, of course).

- The person who will probably read your press release is an editor. It is this person's responsibility to decide whether your event is worth covering and, if so, to assign a specific reporter to the story. Editors read thousands of press releases every year. Think of ways you can make your event and press release different and special. Remember, you only have about 30 seconds to grab the attention of the editors who will read your press release.

Now that you have your press release, to whom should you send it? How do you find and contact the people who would be interested in your cause? Here are some helpful hints:

- Research the news organizations that make up your local media. This may include TV stations, a number of newspapers, magazines, radio stations, and Internet Web sites. You may want to ask your teachers or parents/guardians for their advice.

- It is more difficult (but not impossible) to attract people from non-community media to cover local events. If you can attract a well-known celebrity to your event, or if you plan to do something very special and unique in your campaign, you may want to contact larger media groups to cover your event.

- Collect all the names and phone numbers of the media you want to contact.

- Call the main phone line of each media outlet on your list and ask for the name, phone number, and fax number of the person who covers community news. Be prepared to briefly describe your event to the receptionist.

- Contact the media people first by fax, and then possibly follow up with a phone call. Community reporters often enjoy covering events that young people organize because they are different, unique, and frequently fun.

- If you are holding a fundraiser for an established organization that is active in your local community, such as the Cancer Society or the Humane Society, consider asking them for help with publicity. They may be willing to send your press release to some of their media contacts.

- Believe in yourself and be confident.

On the Day of Your Event

To ensure your event goes as smoothly and professionally as possible, follow some of these helpful hints for dealing with the media:

Before the media arrive...

✔ Designate one person in your group as the media's main contact. This person should be well informed, supplied with written information to hand out, and able to answer questions.

✔ If the conference or event is indoors, use a room that will look filled even if the turnout is small.

✔ Have a media kit on hand to give to reporters. A media kit is essentially the same as a press release kit, with perhaps a few more items added. This kit should contain the following:

- a copy of your media release

- contact names and phone numbers of key people in your group

- information about the issue, such as facts and statistics

- brief biography of the speaker(s) or people of note, such as local politicians or

celebrities, who will be at the event

- photographs, charts, newsletters, or pamphlets, if appropriate (you may want to create some of these specifically for your event)

- endorsements, quotations, and comments (make certain that they are accurate)

✔ Have all necessary material on hand and all equipment checked to ensure it works.

✔ Think of any questions you might be asked and have an idea of how you will answer those questions.

During the interview with the media...

- Be confident. Remember why you organized the event and why you are passionate about your issue. Be energetic and demonstrate the power of your commitment and dedication.

- Look professional and neat.

- Be honest — use only correct statistics and facts. Make certain that you have done your homework and know as much as possible about your issue.

- Use proper English, not slang, when speaking.

- Do not chew gum.

- Smile.

Television is one of the most effective ways to publicize your campaign. It affords you the opportunity to educate thousands (if not millions) of viewers about your issue. Whether you are interviewed on the local community show or on a national talk show, there are a number of things to remember in order to make your television appearance a success. Follow these guidelines when being interviewed on TV:

✔ Always look toward the interviewer and never into the camera itself when answering questions. Pretend that the camera person is invisible.

✔ Do not wear striped clothing or any clothing that is solid white or black. Stripes and solid white and black do not look good on TV. Wear something colorful and youthful.

- Try to keep your answers brief. Short sentences, called *sound bites*, are catchy and powerful statements that work well on television. An example of a sound bite is "Youth are not only the leaders of tomorrow, they are also the leaders of today!"

- Identify beforehand three important components of your event or cause that you want to have broadcast to the world.

- Take a deep breath before you answer the questions. This will help to prevent you from saying "ummmmm" before you respond.

- Ask the interviewer when the interview will be aired on TV.

- Make sure your friends or family videotape the program. You cannot count on receiving tapes from the television station.

- Try to relax and enjoy yourself.

Below are some typical questions the media ask when covering events organized by young people. You may want to think about possible answers to these questions before the event.

- What is this event about? What are you trying to accomplish?

- Why is this issue important to you?

- What has been your greatest challenge thus far in your work?

- There is the common idea that young people only want to hang around malls and play video games. Do you agree? What makes your group different?

- What is the next planned event for your cause?

- What can people do to find out more information about your issue or get involved in your campaign?

- What message do you want to give to the young people who will be watching or reading this interview?

> "Concentrate on where you want to go, not on what you fear."
>
> — **Anthony Robbins**
> **(b. 1960)**
> **Motivational speaker**

Sample Interview with Craig Kielburger

If I Were Mayor...
Craig Kielburger, Child Labor Activist

As Mayor what leader or prominent person would you try to emulate?
I liked Barbara Hall's [former Mayor of Toronto, Ontario] style. It was amazing how she found the time to attend so many community events and how at ease she was with everyone in the city. She was a people's mayor.

Who would be your biggest supporters?
Young people, although they couldn't vote. I would make sure that they would have opportunities to participate in all city activities and to have a voice in issues which affect them.

What would your campaign slogan be?
"Yes, We Can!"

Your campaign song?
"It's a Small World."

Write the first line of your acceptance speech:
It takes a village to raise a child. It also takes a child to help raise a village.

Once in office, what would be your first action?
To create a volunteer youth core program with a stipend for young people who are unemployed or underemployed. I would encourage them to use their energy, enthusiasm and idealism to help improve our city and our communities.

Who would be your closest advisor?
I would need more than one close advisor. When you look at the diversity of the people of Toronto and the influence the city has nationally and internationally, I think that the mayor has to be very careful to have advisors who reflect the complexity of the city. Young people would be well represented.

What three things would you have on your desk?
A picture of my family, my computer and my backgammon game and a special bed for my dog, Muffin, under my desk.

How would your wardrobe change?
I would wear all of my Toronto T-shirts — a different one each day, Maple Leafs, Blue Jays, Raptors, Kids Help Phone, etc. I would inaugurate a casual day across the entire city one day a week at all places of employment with $1 going to local charities.

What is one thing about Toronto that you would most like to change?
I'd like to see more people participate in the decisions being made. I would install a huge suggestion box in city hall and invite the public to drop in their ideas for making the city a better place. Just think of the thousands of good ideas out there not being tapped.

(continued next page)

Sample Interview with Craig Kielburger

What is the one thing you would never change?

I would always want to promote the cultural diversity of the city. Toronto is so unique. It is like the United Nations. I love it! When you travel a lot you learn to appreciate having "the world" in your own city.

What would your political enemies say about you?

They would probably say that I am too young and naive, too idealistic and unprepared for the responsibilities of being mayor. There would be the cynics who would question who is behind me or who is pushing me. Those individuals who believe that youth are not capable of anything but hanging around malls and playing video games.

How would you change the image of Toronto?

I think that it is really sad to see the number of people on the streets of Toronto, homeless and begging. This is a scandal in a rich country like Canada. I know that tourists find it hard to accept. We had a visitor from India who took pictures to "show the people back home." I would like people to think that we have enough compassion and resources to take care of our poor, our homeless and our children in trouble.

How would you improve Toronto's international reputation?

It should be easy. We are an international city. I would work more with the various ethnic groups and the contacts they already have in their countries. I would work with the school boards to twin schools in Toronto with others around the world, not only as a learning experience, but also so that young people can establish contacts and find ways in which they can contribute directly to the global community, especially in poor, developing countries.

What would be the biggest perk to being Mayor?

Having the opportunity to work with other people and to put our ideas in action. We all have our opinions on how we would like to improve our city. Having that opportunity would be the chance of a lifetime.

What lies would you tell to get elected?

I hope that when I reach the point when I start telling lies, I would have the courage and the common sense to quit.

What do you think would be the hardest part of the job?

Putting up with the critics who complain all the time but are never willing to find solutions.

What would you like historians to say about your reign as Mayor?

That I was able to break the stereotype that youth have nothing to contribute to society. I would like to have left the legacy of making Toronto a more humane place where all of its citizens were able to prosper.

"If I Were Mayor" first appeared in the Thornhill Post, March 1998. Reprinted with permission.

Public Service Announcements

Another way to communicate with the public is through public service announcements (PSAs), which are messages about community events or important social issues broadcast on local radio and television stations. A public service announcement is a short commercial or advertisement. As part of their broadcast licensing agreement with the government, most radio and television stations offer 10-, 20-, or 30-second spots for your message free of charge.

Here are some strategies to make the best use of your public service announcement:

✔ Contact your local stations and ask them about specific requirements before you write out your announcement. Do not forget about university and college radio and TV stations, including cable, as they are often an easy way to get your message out to the community.

✔ When you call the radio or TV station, ask to speak to the person who is in charge of public service announcements.

✔ Keep your PSA brief and to the point, as it is often easier to get shorter PSAs on the air.

✔ Start with radio messages first, as they are much easier to create and get broadcast. It is often very difficult to get a public service announcement on TV unless you can find someone who can professionally tape and edit your message. This can be very expensive. If you are uncertain about TV announcements or cannot find any help, stick with radio PSAs.

> " If one is lucky, a single fantasy can totally transform a million realities. "
>
> — Maya Angelou
> (b. 1928)
> Author

Format for a Public Service Announcement

Contact Person:
Full Name
Address
Telephone and Fax Numbers
Date

Necessary Information

- REGARDING: State what your PSA is about.

- TARGET AUDIENCE: Say which groups of people the PSA is hoping to inform (for example, young people, adults).

- AIRING DATES: State when your PSA should start and finish. You do not want your PSA to air after your event is over.

Message

- Make your PSA unique and interesting. Be youthful, but at the same time make certain that you grab the attention of the listeners. You may want to begin with a quick quote or a shocking statistic or fact.

- If your PSA is about an upcoming event, follow the 5Ws+H format (*who*, *what*, *when*, *where*, *why*, and *how*).

- If your PSA is an advertisement to the public, be certain that you

  - state the name of your group

  - state the organization's mission or mandate (what you are trying to accomplish)

  - provide some way listeners can get more information or contact you, such as referring them to your group's Web site, if you have one

End Note

- Do not forget to write *-30-* at the end of your PSA.

- Also indicate the length of time of the PSA in seconds below the message.

–30–

Sample Public Service Announcement

PUBLIC SERVICE ANNOUNCEMENT

Contact Person:
Calvin Michaels
864 Third Street
Madison, WI 67890
Tel: (902) 555-1234
Fax: (902) 555-2222
Cell: (902) 555-2323
cmichaels@hotmail.com

September 25, 20—

REGARDING: Teenagers Against Drunk Driving
TARGET AUDIENCE: Teenagers and young adults
AIRING DATES: Early fall (October 1 to November 30, 20—)

High school graduation is supposed to mark the beginning of a new period in the lives of young people, a time of hopes, dreams, and aspirations for the future. Tragically, all can be lost when someone gets behind the wheel of a car after drinking.

Teenagers Against Drunk Driving is a group of young people who are asking you to drive responsibly. Do not drive if you have been drinking. For more information about our group, please visit our Web site.

-30-
20 seconds

> "Follow your instincts. That's where true wisdom manifests itself.
>
> — Oprah Winfrey (b. 1954) Television talk show host

How to Raise Funds

How to Put the Fun into Fundraising

Raising money to support your cause can be fun, rewarding, and a great way to publicize your cause. The money you raise can be used to fund the basic operating costs of your group, as well as projects that you decide to support.

There are hundreds of ways you can raise money, such as doing odd jobs, selling things, holding a fundraising event, writing proposals to receive grants, obtaining sponsors, and so on.

Sell fundraising items

Often, an easy way to raise money is to sell fundraising items. There are companies listed in the Yellow Pages™ under Fundraising that specialize in merchandise you can sell. Items that you can sell this way include the following:

- prewrapped chocolate bars and candies

- coupon books

- wrapping paper

- magazine subscriptions

- candles

- tinned cookies

Note, however, that a number of such businesses keep a large portion of funds that are raised. Ensure at least half of the money that is raised by selling merchandise goes to your social issue of choice.

Odd jobs

You and your group members can do odd jobs, such as

- mow lawns

- rake leaves

- shovel snow

- wash cars

- walk dogs

- babysit

Tip

For safety reasons, inform your parents/guardians of your intentions before you perform any of these jobs, and only work for people whom you know and trust.

Hold a garage sale

Are you ready to go through your closet and give away some of your old toys, sporting goods, or clothes? Here are some strategies for holding a successful garage sale:

- Ask your family members, including relatives, for donations to your garage sale.

- Ask your neighbors for donations, but make certain that you give them plenty of notice. You may want to advertise with flyers and posters.

- The best time to hold a garage sale is in the spring, summer, or early fall when people are cleaning out their houses and are more likely to be outside.

- Look at the weather reports in advance and try to hold the garage sale when the weather is likely to be good.

- Have other activities at your garage sale, such as children's games, face painting, and refreshments, which can help generate additional funding.

Host a fundraising event at your school

Often, the best place to hold a fundraiser is at your school. Be certain to ask your principal or teacher advisor for permission before you start planning.

Here are 10 school fundraiser ideas:

Pizza lunch: Order pizza and charge each student for every slice they eat. You may want to have people order in advance and pre-pay so you have the right amount of pizza delivered.

Bake sale: Have everyone bake cookies, cakes, brownies, and other goodies, and sell them at lunch to hungry customers.

Barbecue: Hold a lunch or dinner barbecue and charge for burgers and hot dogs. Make certain you also have some veggie hot dogs and burgers for non-meat eaters.

School dance: Organize a dance and charge an entrance fee.

Fashion show: Have local businesses lend seasonal clothes, which can be profiled to young and old alike at a fashion show where proceeds benefit your cause.

Community picnic/dinner: Have local businesses donate food and beverages to be sold at your event, and sell tickets to community members.

Car wash: Wash cars, have a fun water fight, and raise money all at the same time.

Tip

If you go out into your community, make certain that you travel in groups of two or three. It is a good idea to go with an adult as well, as you should never knock on a stranger's door alone.

Movie night: Rent a movie that everyone will enjoy and charge an entrance fee. You might also provide snacks and drinks in exchange for a donation.

Theater night: Have people perform short skits and recite poetry. Ask people at the door for a donation to your cause.

The Budget

Before you begin fundraising, it is a good idea to create a budget that will provide you with information on how much money you will likely spend during your fundraiser and how much money you will collect after your event is over.

You may want to write up a budget that outlines your income (how much you will make) and your expenses (how much you will spend). Try to acquire as many donated items as possible. Ask local businesses if they would be willing to donate materials you need. Tips for donated goods and services are provided on the next few pages.

A simple budget for a car wash might look like the following:

Item	Income (how much you will make)	Expenses (how much you will spend)	Profit (income less expenses)
estimated 50 cars will be washed at $5 per car	$250		
selling of donated drinks at the car wash: 25 cans of soda at $1 each	$25		
buckets and old rags	donated		
location of car wash (old fire hall)	donated		
special car soap: $12 x 2 bottles		$24	
garbage bags: 1 box x $6		$6	
TOTAL	$275	$30	$245

Top 10 Crazy Fundraisers Guaranteed to Work

1. Organize an event. For $1, for example, students could throw a cream pie or water balloon at a willing teacher at lunch hour. Do not forget to get permission from the teacher first!

2. Have a teacher agree to be weighed on a scale. Collect his or her weight in dimes, nickels, and quarters. For example, if your teacher weighs 180 pounds, collect 180 pounds of coins. Collect donations in the form of change from your peers, community members, and adult supporters.

3. Organize a school car wash in which teachers agree to participate in a water fight.

4. Have a doughnut-eating contest and charge contestants an entry fee. Try to get jelly doughnuts donated by a local store in exchange for recognition of their involvement.

5. Hold a rock-a-thon. Get a group of students together who will stay up all night in your school's gym rocking on rocking chairs. Before you start the event, collect pledges for every hour you spend rocking. Organize fun games and activities you can do at night while seated. Use your imagination.

6. Find a teacher or principal who would be willing to have his or her head shaved in front of the entire school if your group reaches its funding goal.

7. Organize a Taste of the Nations lunch or dinner. Set up tables representing various countries (put a flag on each table to identify the nation) and serve food from that region of the world (such as Italian, Indian, Greek, Chinese, and Mexican). Charge people to participate in the lunch or dinner event.

8. Hold a contest whereby participants pay a fee to try their luck at matching baby photos

with your group members or teachers. The winner gets a prize. Try to get a donated prize to give away.

9. Ask permission from your teacher or principal to hold a contest whereby the lucky winner will receive one day free from homework.

10. Sponsor a dunk tank. Ask students, teachers, and the principal to take a turn on the hot seat. Note that it can be expensive to rent a dunk tank, so make sure beforehand that interest is sufficient enough to result in a profit.

101 Fundraisers

If you are looking for more fundraising ideas, take a look at the following 101 Fundraising suggestions. These ideas are designed to trigger your imagination. Do not forget to think about safety concerns as you make your plans, such as seeking permission where necessary, and informing parents/guardians and teachers of your plans. The most important thing is to have fun.

1. **Jellybean count:** Fill a jar with jellybeans and have people pay to guess how many there are in the jar.

2. **Dress-down/casual day:** If you attend a school that requires a uniform, have a day on which all the students can wear casual clothes. Charge each student who wants to participate. Make certain that you ask permission from your principal first.

3. **Band and choir concerts:** Ask your school band or choir to donate their time by performing a benefit concert for your cause. Charge admission for the event.

4. **Walkathon:** Choose a date and a route, make up some pledge forms, and advertise with posters. Have everyone who wants to participate gather donations or pledges using their pledge forms.

5. **Bag groceries:** Ask a local grocery store if you can bag people's groceries for donations. Be certain to put up a sign saying what the donation is for.

6. **Skip-a-thon:** Choose a date, make up pledge forms, and advertise with posters. Have everyone who wants to participate gather donations or pledges using their pledge forms, and then skip.

7. **Raffles:** Sell tickets and keep ticket stubs. On the date of the draw, have someone close his or her eyes and pick a ticket stub from all the ones that were sold. Do this publicly. The winner receives a prize.

8. **Auction:** Have individuals, groups, and businesses donate goods and services. Be creative in what you can auction off and make certain that the goods and services are sold at reasonable prices.

9. **Perform a free service for donations:** Rake leaves, shovel snow, take care of a pet. When offering your service, ask the person who benefited from your actions for a donation toward your worthy cause.

10. **Sell candy or cards:** Work with reputable businesses that provide merchandise you can sell. Be sure at least half of the money raised goes to your cause.

11. **Winter carnival:** Hold a winter carnival in your local park or schoolyard. Invite students, staff, and the community. Charge admission and/or a small fee to play games.

12. **Carnival day:** Host a mini-carnival, with games, prizes, and popcorn, in a local park or your own backyard. Charge admission and/or a small fee to play games.

13. **Spelling bee:** Look through some books or in the dictionary and come up with a list of words of increasing difficulty. Have participants and spectators pay to participate.

14. **Battle of the bands:** Gather some bands from your local community. Book a venue and advertise with posters, flyers, and radio announcements. Hold a mini-concert in which the audience chooses the winning band.

15. **Pitch-a-thon:** Rent a radar gun and measure how fast people can throw a baseball or kick a soccer ball. Charge $1 per try and give a prize to the fastest individual.

16. **Sell buttons or T-shirts displaying your logo:** Create a logo, and then make up a whole bunch of T-shirts, buttons, pens, or other gifts with your logo on them. Sell the items at a reasonable price.

17. **Puppet show:** Make puppets with socks, felt, and other craft materials. Pick out or write a story. Set a date, time, and location. Advertise with flyers and posters. Sell tickets in advance and at the door.

18. **Spaghetti dinner:** Prepare a great dinner for students, teachers, or community members and charge a fee.

19. **Hold a theme party:** Decide on a fun theme. Charge an entrance fee, but be sure to explain to people what their cover charge is going toward.

20. **Newsletter:** Create a newsletter informing your peers and members of your community about your organization or cause. Sell the newsletter for a small fee. Be sure to provide information about how people can become involved and/or donate to your cause.

21. **Plant a tree:** Ask a nursery for seedling donations and then get people to sponsor a tree.

22. **Pledges:** Gather pledges to have dance-a-thons, rock-a-thons, or any other type of endurance contest you can think of.

23. **Day of community service:** Gather together a group of friends, and contact a number of organizations for which you would be interested in volunteering. Then have people sponsor you to do community service for 24 hours.

24. **Food fast:** Get together with a group of friends, gather pledges, and fast for a full 24 hours.

25. **Piñata contest:** Charge a fee to have each blindfolded person have one turn at trying to break a candy-filled piñata.

26. **Craft sale:** Make all the crafts yourself and sell them.

27. **Geography bee:** Organize a spelling bee composed of geographical names from around the world. Participants should obtain sponsors for their correct answers.

28. **Family barbecue:** Host a family barbecue in your backyard, with games and activities.

29. **Three-on-three basketball tournament:** Organize a basketball tournament in your school with the winning team receiving a prize. This can also be done with soccer, tennis, badminton, or any other sport.

30. **Swim-a-thon:** Get sponsors for the number of laps you swim.

31. **Beat the goalie:** Pick the best hockey or soccer goalie you know and invite people to try to score a goal for a prize. Every participant has to pay to play.

32. **Bingo:** Host a bingo night at a local hall, place of worship, or school.

33. **Plant sale:** Organize a plant sale with plants donated by local nurseries.

34. **Games night:** Organize an evening of board games.

35. **Boat race:** Organize a model boat race on a body of water. Charge a participant/spectator entrance fee. The winner of the race gets a prize.

36. **Fruit stand:** Get permission to go to local farms and pick fruit to sell. Sell the produce in high-traffic areas or at community festivals.

37. **Book sale:** Ask all your friends, relatives, and teachers to donate their old books. Advertise your book sale by means of posters and flyers. Set up a table and sell books. If there are leftovers, you can always give them to a needy library, shelter, or school.

38. **Bowling:** Organize a bowling night or a competition. Charge everyone a small fee to enter or have participants get bowl-a-thon pledges.

39. **Buy a brick:** If you are fundraising to build a school or building, have people make donations to purchase bricks.

40. **Petting zoo:** If you live in an area in which there are farms nearby, organize a one-day petting zoo for children.

41. **Coupon sale:** Have coupon books donated by local businesses, and then sell them to students and adults.

42. **International dinner:** Have people from various ethnic origins cook traditional foods, and then charge admission to an international dinner.

43. **Balloon pop:** Before filling a balloon with air or helium, put a note inside. Have a certain number of the notes worth a prize. Have people buy balloons and pop them in the hope of getting the prize. Be sure to pick up the broken balloons afterward.

44. **Scavenger hunt:** Set a route and make a list of items that the participants need to find in order to win. Advertise your scavenger hunt well and charge everyone a small fee to participate. The winning person/group gets a prize.

45. **Car wash:** With a group of friends, set up a car wash in the parking lot of your school, church, or public area. (Be sure to ask for permission and make sure that people are careful of moving cars.)

46. **Carol-singing:** During the Christmas season, go door-to-door singing carols for donations. It is a good idea to have a card or a flyer with some brief information about your organization to give to sponsors. You may want to have an adult accompany you. Remember to respect those who do not celebrate Christmas and who may not want to hear your carols.

47. **Candle-making:** Make candles and sell them to family members. This can be educational and fun, but be sure to exercise all safety precautions.

48. **Hug-a-gram:** Advertise a hug for a dollar. Have people buy a hug for a friend. After a member of your group gives the hug to the designated person, give them a small card with a message from the person who sent the hug.

49. **Sporting events tickets:** Ask sports teams to donate a number of seats for their games and raffle off the tickets.

50. **Charity ball:** Hire a DJ or a band, rent a hall, advertise, and sell tickets for a dance.

51. **Christmas ornament sale:** Sell Christmas ornaments during the Christmas season.

52. **Classic car show:** Organize a classic automobile show. Invite people to attend and to bring their cars by placing ads in local newspapers, leaving flyers at local businesses, and charging people to come and see the show.

53. Miniature golf: Build a nine-hole miniature golf course at your school, featuring ramps, water and sand traps, and other obstacles. Charge people to play a round during lunch.

54. Bench-a-thon: Have people bench press weights in the school gym and collect pledges for every pound they lift. This is a popular event, especially with football players. Make sure all participants have spotters to ensure safety.

55. Clearing snow: Shovel snow from people's driveways and walkways in the winter months for a donation.

56. Monopoly match: Have a group of students play a Monopoly tournament with the winner receiving a prize.

57. Guess the age of your teacher: Organize an event in which students pay to guess the age of your teacher. Obtain approval from your teacher first, however.

58. Hoopla: The competitor throws hoops over prizes. The person whose hoop completely lands over the prize gets to keep the award. Make sure you do not spend too much money on prizes.

59. Pumpkin-decorating contest: Around Halloween, hold a pumpkin-decorating contest among different grades of homerooms.

60. Debate evening: Research a number of debate issues and invite various community members to debate issues. Charge the audience to come and watch. The issues can be fun. For example, have your school principal argue that listening to music during class enhances a student's ability to learn versus a student who thinks that music should be banned from school.

61. Dog show: Invite people to show off their dogs in a show. Make it a competition that people pay to enter, and offer a prize for the best groomed dog, most- and least-obedient dog, and so on.

62. Talent auction: Auction off the talents of people. For instance, great singers offer to sing at a wedding, party, or special event.

63. Duck race: Sell numbered plastic ducks. Set all the ducks afloat in a race on a river. The person who bought the duck that wins the race gets a prize.

64. Guess the number of coins in a jar: The winner receives all the coins and your group makes money charging people for guessing.

65. Comedy hour: Host a comedy skit during lunch at your school and charge people to attend.

66. Nacho party: Plan a morning to make nachos and popcorn, which can be sold during lunch.

67. **Eating marathon:** Have a pie-eating, hot-dog eating, or ice cream-eating contest. You can charge people to participate or to watch, or you can make all participants obtain pledges.

68. **Face painting:** Have a face-painting day. Advertise in advance and then charge a small fee for painting young kids' faces during a school day or on a weekend.

69. **Ugly tie contest:** Have the students come to school wearing the ugliest tie they can find. Have them vote on the worst tie with the winner receiving a prize.

70. **Flower show:** Invite gardeners from your community to enter their flowers in a competition for a prize. Ask volunteer experts to be judges and charge all participants and spectators a fee.

71. **Calendar sale:** Create a calendar highlighting the projects and members of your organization, and sell it to students and their family members.

72. **Sports tournament/fitness competition:** Organize a sports tournament or fitness competition. Advertise well and charge spectators to come and watch groups compete. You may need to have medical personnel on hand.

73. **Crazy hat day:** Have students pay a fee to wear a crazy hat to school for the day.

74. **"Get-out-of-jail-free" card:** Pay to get out of a class period for a day. Ask permission from your teachers or principal first.

75. **Art sale:** Have local artists donate some of their works, which will be displayed and then sold to the public.

76. **Game show:** Recreate one or more of your favorite game shows and charge contestants a small entrance fee. Sell tickets to the audience.

77. **Gardening:** Tend the garden of a neighbor, a local store, or community park for a donation.

78. **Guest speaker:** Invite a guest speaker to your home or local hall and sell admission tickets to raise funds for your cause.

79. **Karaoke:** Rent a karaoke machine, sell tickets or charge an admission fee, and sing all night.

80. **Videos:** Make and sell a video for youth tourists of places to go and cool things to do. Or create a How-To video; for example, how to improve your golf swing, or how to make crafts.

81. **Mile of coins:** Gather donations of coins (pennies, dimes, or quarters) and lay them side by side until they stretch out to be a mile long. Alternatively, surround your school gym, library, or parking lot with the coins.

82. **Recipe book:** Gather together favorite recipes and put them together in a book. Sell the book through your school, sports organization, or community center. Try to get the photocopying donated by local businesses.

83. **Sit in a bath:** Obtain sponsorship for kids to sit in a bath of something gross and out of the ordinary, such as baked beans or fruit-flavored gelatin.

84. **Talent show competition:** Invite people to show off their talent in a competition in which they can win a prize. Sell tickets in advance.

85. **Henna hand art:** Find out if any members of your group know how to apply henna (Indian hand art), which can be applied to people in your school for a fee.

86. **Walk dogs:** Love pets? Try walking dogs every day for a fee.

87. **Toy sale:** Hold a toy sale. The best season for this is just prior to Christmas.

88. **Triathlon:** Set a course of running, cycling, and swimming. Have participants get pledges to compete to win prizes.

89. **Lemonade stand:** Make lemonade, post signs, and sell it on a hot day.

90. **January:** Snow art contest.

91. **February:** Valentine's Day dance; red carnations for Valentine's Day.

92. **March:** St. Patrick's Day party; spring car wash.

93. **April:** Spring flower sale.

94. **May:** Mother's Day flower sale.

95. **June:** Father's Day sale; end-of-school pool party (with lifeguards).

96. **July:** Fourth of July festivities with refreshment/food booths.

97. **August:** End-of-summer party.

98. **September:** Back-to-school dance; back-to-school supplies sale.

99. **October:** Halloween party; pumpkin sales.

100. **November:** Thanksgiving turkey raffle.

101. **December:** Christmas tree sale; gift-wrapping service; New Year's Eve babysitting.

Ask the Community to Help

Obtaining community help is a great way to minimize the cost of your fundraising event. Ask for donated products and services that you can use as prizes, such as the following:

✔ Have a local photocopying business agree to copy your flyers for free.

✔ A computer company might donate a computer for the use of your group.

✔ A trophy store might donate a trophy for your group to give to the winner of a contest.

✔ Local stores could donate prizes to be given away.

Keep in mind some of these helpful hints when asking businesses for donations:

✔ Have a letter of introduction explaining to the business who you are and why you are asking for donations. Be sure to explain to the business how the donations will be used.

✔ Familiarize yourself with preparing a suitable proposal as some companies may specify the need for one before they can consider your request. See page 80 for tips on writing proposals.

✔ Whether you are writing a donation letter or a proposal, try to build a relationship with the business representative. Have the same person from your group communicate with the business. Have your parents/guardians suggest names of businesses to approach. Some will be businesses they know and deal with.

✔ Ask for donations early. Sometimes businesses have to get permission from an owner or a head office.

✔ Invite a representative from the business to your event and thank them publicly for the donation.

✔ Let people know which companies and individuals made donations by putting this information on posters and flyers. It is a nice way to say thank you.

✔ Once the fundraising project is complete, send out thank-you letters and write a report outlining how much money the group generated. If a business makes a donation once, it is likely to make one again, but only if it feels its contribution was appreciated and sufficiently acknowledged. Keep a record of the business name, what it gave as a donation, to whom you spoke, and any other important facts you can remember.

> " The mind is the limit. As long as your mind can envision the fact that you can do something, you can do it. "
>
> — Arnold Schwarzenegger (b. 1947) Actor

How to Write a Donation Letter

Writing a donation letter can be an easy way to let local businesses know about your group and how they can help by providing donated goods and services. In your donation letter, you will want to include the following:

✔ Information about your group and its mission.

✔ An explanation of the project or event that you are organizing.

✔ The type of donation you are seeking from the business.

✔ The type of recognition the business can expect to receive from you for the donation.

✔ Other donations you require. This is extremely important because the business representative may have contacts with other businesses that can provide the additional goods or services you need.

✔ A statement of thanks for their time and attention. Tell them that you look forward to hearing from them soon.

Be sure to follow up no later than one week after the letter has been sent, either by visiting the business in person or by making a phone call to the company.

Sample Donation Letter

Jean Boulanger
863 Lemay Avenue
Modesto, CA 78910
(213) 555-2323

September 5, 20—

Ms. Elaine Silver
Juice Beverages Inc.
454 Rowanwood Blvd.
Modesto, CA 78910

Dear Ms. Silver,

My name is Jean Boulanger. I am in the tenth grade at Greely High School. I work with an organization called Health for All. We are a youth organization whose mission is to help raise awareness of AIDS and donate money for research. As you may know, there were 3 million HIV/AIDS-related deaths in the year 2000 alone. Five hundred thousand of those who died were children.

We are organizing a walkathon on October 15 to raise money for our group. We are seeking the support of Juice Beverages Inc. to donate 10 cases of juice as refreshments for the event. We would be happy to high-light the name and logo of Juice Beverages Inc. on all the promotional material that will be distributed for the event, as well as thank Juice Beverages Inc. publicly at the opening ceremonies of the walkathon.

We also require donated cups and food items. If you know of companies that might be interested in supporting our event, please get back to me. We hope to be able to raise $3,000 to donate toward AIDS research.

Thank you for your time and consideration. If you have any questions, please do not hesitate to contact me. I look forward to hearing from you.

Sincerely,

Jean Boulanger

Jean Boulanger

How to Write a Proposal

Proposals are another way to communicate your ideas and provide others with information on what you are trying to accomplish. When asking for donated materials, some companies ask for a proposal providing a full explanation about your group and how the donated goods will be used.

Format for a Proposal

Title
(Give your proposal a catchy title in the center of the top of the page. Try to grab the attention of the reader).

- **To:** State the name and address of the person or group to whom the proposal is being presented.

- **From:** State your name, full address, and phone and fax numbers.

- **Date:** Make certain that you write a date on your proposal.

- Briefly explain the mission of your group. What are you trying to accomplish? It is a good idea to include the name of an adult supervisor, such as a teacher, in case the company wishes to contact another reference. Provide phone numbers or email addresses for any reference(s) you list.

- State what it is that you want from the foundation or the company.

- State how the foundation or company will be recognized for its donation.

- **List the items required:** Show the reader that you have done your homework and have thought about what you will need to put your plan into action. This is really important because the business representative may have contacts with other businesses that can provide the additional goods or services you require.

Kids Making Kits

To: Mr. John Halford; Store Manager of The Gift Store
From: Christine Huang
       35 Oakridge Road
       Brady, TX 89101

April 14, 20—

Our Group:

    Teens Taking Action is a youth group based in Brady dedicated to making the world a better place through community service projects and programs. Our mission is to help make our city a happier, more caring community. The teacher who serves as a mentor for the Group is Mrs. Barton, who can be reached by phone at 555-6768, or by email at barton@hotmail.com.

The Idea:

    Teens Taking Action proposes a day of fun and community service. We would like to spend a day making gift baskets for senior citizens to show them that we care. This is important to us because we feel that senior citizens add a great deal to our community life. We think that this would be a nice way to say "thank you" for all of the guidance and support they have given to young people. The gift baskets will be handed out at the Parkview Retirement Home.

The Request:

    We would like The Gift Store to donate forty (40) medium-sized gift baskets, which we can fill with other donated products, as well as drawings and letters.

Recognition:

- Teens Taking Action would be more than happy to tell the recipients all about the generous donation from The Gift Store.

- The logo and address of The Gift Store will be highlighted on the Teens Taking Action Web site.

- Teens Taking Action will send out a press release about the project to local media and highlight the sponsorship of The Gift Store in the materials.

Other Requirements:

    Teens Taking Action requires other materials to make this project a success. If you or your company know of any other business that we might approach to donate any of the following items, please let me know:

- hand cream, shampoo, and soap

- decks of playing cards

- fruits, cookies, and snacks

Tip

Do not be discouraged if your proposal is not chosen. Ask for feedback from the company or foundation so that you might improve your next proposal.

Grants and Foundations

A grant is a donation to be used for a specific group or project. To receive a grant, you have to submit a proposal to the group offering the grant.

Foundations are private groups that donate money to various causes. You often need charitable status from the federal government to receive money from foundations; however, there are some small community foundations that will give money to local causes and groups. You will have to write a proposal to the foundation if you hope to receive funding this way.

Large corporations sometimes give grants. You can make it a group project to contact a number of corporations. Ask someone in the public relations department of various corporations whether the company sponsors any grants.

Grants are often difficult to get, so do not expect them to be your main source of funding. However, it is worth trying because the amount of money you may receive can be quite large compared to the amount you would raise in a normal fundraising event.

Each foundation has its own requirements for grant proposals. Contact the program officer of the foundation to find out if your group is eligible for funding.

> **"Only those who dare to fail greatly can ever achieve greatly."**
>
> — **Robert F. Kennedy**
> **(1925–1968)**
> **United States senator**

PART 3
Where You Can Get Involved
— Everywhere!

Being committed to positive change doesn't mean you have to take on the whole world. You can get involved wherever you find the need for change or the opportunity to help others. Look around you. Do you see anything at school, around your home, or in your community that could be helped or improved? Challenge yourself to think creatively and constructively about the world. Develop concrete ways to make it a more positive place. Remember that you have both a right and a responsibility to help find solutions to problems that touch your life and the lives of your peers. There are many ways that you can make a difference, and your every contribution counts.

At Home

Your actions to make the world a better place can begin in your own home. It is important that you respect and show concern for the quality of life of others. Whatever your family arrangements, you can help out with some of the work that needs to be done on a daily basis. The people with whom you live will be grateful because your contributions will be making a difference to your home environment.

Here are a few ways to help out around your home:

✔ Help clear the table.

✔ Do the dishes.

✔ Do the vacuuming.

✔ Help younger brothers and sisters with their homework.

✔ Babysit.

✔ Take care of your pets. Feed them regularly, and make sure they always have fresh water, exercise, and lots of love.

✔ Return library books for other family members.

✔ Shovel snow or clear ice.

✔ Help with the laundry.

✔ Try to help other members of your family, such as grandparents, aunts, uncles, and cousins. They may appreciate a visit as much as anything, but remember to arrange it ahead of time.

You can probably think of many more ways to make a positive contribution to your home. Make a list and start surprising your family.

Plan a family-Togetherness Activity

Households can be very busy and even hectic. With each member of the family involved in his or her own activities, it can be difficult to find time to spend together. Taking some time to enjoy one another's company can help keep a family feeling connected.

Choose an idea

Talk to your family members or the other people with whom you live. How much time does everyone have? A day? An evening? Will you stay in or go out? Determine the types of activities that every family member prefers and then choose to do something that appeals to everyone. Here are some fun ideas that many people enjoy:

- ✔ a pizza and movie night
- ✔ a picnic
- ✔ a walk or hike
- ✔ a night of board games or cards
- ✔ a family football, soccer, hockey, basketball, or baseball game

There are lots of other things you can do. Be creative and open to suggestions. The most important thing is that you all have fun together. With any activity, planning is an important part of the process.

Choose a date

Once again, talk to everyone involved to determine some possible dates and times for your activity. Choose a date when everyone is free and plan it well in advance so that everybody can participate.

Decide who will participate

You may want to include other people in your activity, such as grandparents or cousins. All family members should make this decision together.

Do not forget!

Leave reminders for everyone. Make colorful notes and post them on the refrigerator, on a house bulletin board, or on bedroom doors.

Enjoy your activity

Enjoy one another's company. Thank everyone for participating, and gather ideas for the next activity.

Tip

If you are including people who do not live in your home, think of a way to remind them about the activity. You might phone or email them, or mail them a note.

At School

The possibilities for involvement at school are endless. Your school is filled with amazing people who have various talents and interests. Getting together and getting involved will lead to a lot of new friendships. Always speak with a teacher or to your principal to get permission before you start any projects, and try to get them involved as well.

Here are some ideas to get you started:

- Be a friend to new students at your school. Show them around and introduce them to your friends and teachers. By being a friend, you will gain a friend yourself and you will also improve your communication and interpersonal skills.

- Help out with younger classes. Young children admire older students. You can do fun and educational activities, such as reading, drawing, or painting. Help younger students do their homework and develop your presentation and communication skills at the same time.

- Organize a fundraising event to finance school activities. In the process, you will develop your organizational skills and inspire others through teamwork.

- Encourage school spirit by organizing an activity of the month, such as school dances, fashion shows, sporting events, or games. Discover how you, too, can work with the media and inform people about fun activities.

- Become a student representative. If your school does not have a student government, talk to a teacher or your principal about starting one. You will become a better public speaker in the process.

- Become a journalist for your school newspaper, or a disc jockey for your school radio station. If your school does not have a newspaper or radio station, talk to your teacher or principal about starting one. Such great activities help you to become a critical thinker, a proficient writer, and a better researcher.

- Work as a peer tutor, counsellor, or mentor. You can participate in conflict mediation, helping to settle disputes in a fair way, or listen when fellow students need someone to talk to. You will need training to do these things. Does your school offer any of these programs? If not, you may want to talk to your guidance counselor or principal about the idea. By doing so, you will become a great listener and perhaps a close friend.

- Promote after-school safety. Raise awareness among students about crosswalk and school bus safety, as well as home safety. Presenting a plan of action to implement the after-school safety program will give you valuable experience with running an effective meeting.

Encourage School Spirit with Spirit Week

Spirit Week is intended to get people involved in school activities and to be proud of their school. Encourage everybody to participate. Try to come up with activities that appeal to a variety of interests. This will help you draw out different groups of students from all over your school, and get them excited about getting involved.

Choose an issue

Decide what you want to accomplish with Spirit Week and the best way to go about it. Is there a specific message you want to get across to your classmates, or a theme that you know would unite them? Think of what your whole school could accomplish once Spirit Week has inspired and motivated every student. In what direction could you focus all that positive energy to do something productive as a team?

Do your research

Ask your teacher or principal to get involved in a Spirit Week. Request their advice, and that of your student government leaders, for ways to organize one. Discuss possible dates with your principal and student leaders. Make sure the date you choose will not conflict with other activities that are already planned, such as a career week or a sports tournament.

Build a team

You can accomplish a lot on your own, but it will require the efforts of a team to make Spirit Week happen. The more people who are involved in planning, the more ideas there will be. The workload can be divided among the team members so no one person is overwhelmed with tasks.

Call a meeting

Speak to your friends and classmates and let them know about Spirit Week. Encourage them to get involved and to help you develop a plan of action. You may also want to solicit some input from teachers and your principal. Set a date to gather your team members to discuss the issues.

Make a plan of action

Here are a few items you will need to discuss:

- What will be the theme or main events of Spirit Week? For example, you might have everyone dress up according to a different theme on each day of Spirit Week: Pajama Day, Backwards Day, Inside-Out Day, Crazy Hat Day, Beach Day, just to name a few. Alternatively, encourage all the clubs and organizations in the school to do something to show people what they are about. You can hold a general assembly with speeches, music, and school chants. If you have a school band, they may want to play at the assembly. You could even invite local celebrities to attend.

- Are you planning to reach out into the community? While everyone is in the spirit, try to think of ways you can use Spirit Week to show your community that the students in your school care. For example, you could hold a food drive as part of Spirit Week and arrange to deliver the goods you collect to the food bank.

- How will you advertise Spirit Week? Advertise your event by making large, colorful posters and flyers. Put an announcement in the school newspaper. Remind people about Spirit Week over your school's public announcement system (with permission, of course). Try other ways you can think of to let people know about your event.

Take action and then review

Coordinating a Spirit Week is challenging, but if there are plenty of volunteers, it will be lots of fun. Enjoy all of the activities.

At the end of Spirit Week, bring your team together and talk about the good points of the event, as well as some lessons that were learned in order to make other Spirit Weeks even better. You may want to create a checklist to use for your next Spirit Week.

Have fun!

Have fun while organizing Spirit Week and enjoy strengthening the spirit and energy of your school. After your event has been successfully completed, hold a celebration or host a party to thank all of your team members.

Take Action to Give Students Power

Becoming involved at school can give you and your fellow students a voice and power in issues that concern you. Here are some ideas for such projects:

- Involve the student body in writing a Constitution for the student government.

- Involve the student body in writing a Charter of Student Rights and Responsibilities.

- Take action to have a student representative on the local school board and the Parent–Teacher Association or school council.

- Work with your local government representative to set up a youth council for your community, your state, or your country.

Start a Club with a Purpose

Starting a club with a purpose is a great way of gathering a group of students who share a common passion, and directing their joint energy towards a specific goal. When group members choose a collective goal and focus all of their unique strengths towards it, there is no limit to what can be accomplished. A club with a purpose not only cultivates passion and energy around a shared cause, it also helps everyone involved think creatively and purposefully about the things they care about.

Helping hands club

- Decide who is in need in your community and then organize events that will benefit them. For example, organize a toy sale. Use the profits you make to buy new toys for children in need, or to buy gifts for residents of nursing homes.

- Organize a food drive to aid a local food bank.

> " To accomplish great things we must not only act, but also dream; not only plan, but also believe! "
>
> — Anatole France (1844–1924) Writer and critic

Environmental club

- Clean up your environment at school. You and your friends can pick up litter on school grounds and cover up graffiti. Get permission from a teacher first, and never touch any broken glass or needles. Promote recycling. Get permission to start a garden or a compost pile behind the school building.

- Organize a garbage-free lunch. Encourage students to store food in reusable plastic containers and to pack lunches in reusable cloth bags. Encourage everyone to make garbage-free lunches a habit and the amount of garbage in landfills will decline.

Debating club

- Choose topics from current events, and have people represent different sides of an issue. Try representing the side you do not agree with. You will educate yourself about important issues and learn to understand other people's points of view.

Human rights club

- You and your friends can join organizations that are concerned with human rights (see Part 5 for contact information).

- Have individual members research various human rights issues, and then convene the group to share the results.

- Hold fundraising events to support your cause.

- Invite guest speakers to your school. (You will need to involve the principal in this endeavor.) Guest speakers could include such people as city councilors, congressmen, experts in various fields, or anyone who you think has an interesting message.

In Your Community

There are many ways to get involved in your community. Keep your eyes open when you are riding your bike or walking around the area where you live. Is there a food bank? Are there any seniors' residences? Is there a park for children? Is there graffiti on the walls of the neighborhood buildings? Are there trees? Are the streets clean?

A real community values every member for her or his contribution. People work together to make the community a good place for everyone.

There are plenty of things you can do to make a difference in your community. Here are a few suggestions

- Organize a neighborhood barbecue or a community garage sale for charity. Encourage everybody to come out and get to know the neighbors.

- Create a Neighborhood Watch system for kids, or introduce a Block Parents program.

- Get involved in land preservation. Is there a piece of land in your area that you think should stay as green space? Write letters and petitions to try to prevent developers from building on it.

- Start a neighborhood beautification program and involve other young people. Paint fences and clean up graffiti. Pick up litter in vacant lots, playgrounds and parks, and around streams and lakes. Always get permission from an adult, and never touch broken glass, needles, or condoms.

- Help elderly neighbors with chores, such as shopping for groceries, mowing lawns, pulling weeds, or shoveling snow. They will appreciate the help, and will also enjoy your company.

After a day of helping out in your community, gather your team together and have some fun to celebrate the contributions you have made. When you end the day feeling great about your work, you and your friends will be inspired to continue making a difference.

WHERE YOU CAN GET INVOLVED— EVERYWHERE!

Organize a Drive

Holding a drive can draw together an entire community. When you organize a drive for food, clothes, or other important supplies, you make those who are more fortunate aware of the problems within their community, and provide them with a way to take part in a concrete solution. At the same time, you are helping the less fortunate understand that they are not alone and that their community is working to help improve their lives. A drive can teach the organizers, participants, and the people in need that every small contribution makes a difference.

Choose an issue

Organizing a drive is a great way to serve your community. You might find yourself in need at some point in your life, so it is your duty as a citizen to do what you can to assist those who are hungry, homeless, or impoverished. When you support services such as food banks and shelters for the homeless, you are demonstrating to the people who use them that their community cares.

Do your research

✔ Ask officials at community food banks or shelters if they would like you to hold a drive. If so, determine what their greatest area of need is; for example, winter clothing, canned food items, shoes, sleeping bags, and so on.

✔ Find out how you can organize such a drive. Involve an adult sponsor if you need one. Choose a school or community event that you can take advantage of, and request permission from the organizers to piggyback your drive on their event. For example, if you want to hold the drive in conjunction with a school concert, ask the principal to become involved.

Build a team

Tell your friends and neighbors about the drive and determine how they can help. There are many things that need to come together in order to organize a successful campaign.

Call a meeting

Speak to your team and seek their advice on how to proceed. Assign roles and responsibilities.

Make a plan of action

Here are a few things you will need to decide:

✔ How will you let people know about your drive? You could, for example, advertise your food drive in the school and in the community. If the drive is part of a special event, let

> " We live surrounded by a sea of poverty. Nevertheless, this sea can decrease in size. Our work is only a drop in the bucket, but this drop is necessary. "
>
> **— Mother Theresa (1910–1997) Catholic nun**

people know that the event and drive are happening at the same time so they will remember to bring items for your drive. One idea is to have a donated item serve as admission for the event, such as for a dance or movie night.

✔ Make eye-catching flyers and posters. Send an announcement to the local newspaper. Inform the student body during morning announcements. Can you think of other ways to let people know about the event and your special drive?

✔ How will you hold the donations: in large boxes, bins, or baskets?

✔ Where will you put the bins?

✔ How will you transport the donations to the food bank after the event?

✔ What other logistical requirements do you need to work out?

Take action and then review

Follow through with all of your actions and have a back-up plan in place, just in case. Do not leave anything to chance. If the boxes fill up, make sure there are always others handy for more donations.

Donate the goods. Bring the food, clothes, shoes, and other items that you have received to the food bank or shelter.

Thank all organizers of the event for their cooperation in making the drive a success. Also thank the people who made donations and encourage them to donate to the shelter or food bank throughout the year.

Soon after the drive, bring your team together and share what was good about the event, as well as any lessons that were learned so that future drives can be better planned and executed.

Have fun!

Have fun organizing the drive and take pride in knowing that you are helping to relieve the suffering of people in your community.

A Rally or a Forum

When you organize a rally or a forum, you are creating a space for people to communicate their ideas freely and share their visions for positive change. When people are given the opportunity to express their knowledge and feelings about a cause, their passion can inspire and motivate an entire crowd to take action. You can organize a rally or a forum relating to a particular cause or theme important to your community and invite speakers to relay their thoughts, personal experiences, and messages to the public.

> "You miss 100% of the shots you never take.
>
> — Wayne Gretzky (b. 1961)
> Athlete

Points to consider:

1. What jobs have to be done in preparation for the event? During the event? After the event?

2. Location
- What is a good location?
- Is it the right size? (Not too big, but not too small.)
- Is the location accessible by public transportation?
- Are washroom facilities available?
- What is the cost? Is a permit necessary?

3. Responsibilities
- Who will be the key person in charge?
- Whom can we ask to speak at the event?

- Are there important individuals who might participate? Who will invite/meet the speakers?
- Who will be the master of ceremonies?
- Will there be music at the event? Who will organize it?
- Who will be responsible for advertising the event?
- What equipment is necessary?
- How will the event be advertised?
- Who will prepare the press release?
- Who will handle the press?
- Who will be responsible for cleaning up?
- Who will send thank-you letters?

4. Logistics/Money
- How will we raise the money to sponsor the event?
- Whom can we ask to contribute donations to the event?
- Who will be responsible for finances?
- Will we have a display at the event? A sign?
- Who will set up the display? Who will make the sign?
- Who will distribute literature at the event?
- At what time will the organizers meet?
- At what time will the event begin?

Now that you have asked yourself all of these questions, do not get discouraged. Rallies or forums can be a great success if done well. Begin to delegate to your team members various areas of responsibility and encourage them to exercise their leadership capabilities. It is also recommended that you find an adult who is familiar with organizing such events to serve as a mentor for you and your team.

More Actions to Take to Get Your Message Across

Once you have educated yourself on an issue, you have both a right and a responsibility to share your knowledge and passion with the people around you. When your community sees how strongly you feel about your cause, they may be inspired and motivated to join your campaign. Be creative when you are trying to get your point across. People will remember what you have said if you can phrase your message in a unique and exciting way.

Street theater

One of the most popular means of educating the public in the developing world is through street theater. Groups perform skits, sing, read stories, recite poetry, or use puppets to create awareness of issues affecting youth. You may want to try these ideas in a public place — for example, at your school or at a rally. Depending on the location you choose, you may have to obtain permission first.

March

March or walk down the street, to your school, to city hall, or across the park. Marches or walks may be used simply to educate the public or to raise funds for your cause. If you are planning a large march, it is recommended that you contact the police ahead of time to inform them of your plans and to inquire if there are any laws, restrictions, or permits required. Make sure that parents/guardians or teachers are aware of your intentions.

Organize carefully where your group will march and how you will publicize the event. Set up a calling tree to invite as many young people as possible to participate in your march. Have a sign-in table to take the names of the participants for future activities. You may want to carry signs to deliver a message to the public. You may also consider using walkie-talkies or cell phones so that the leaders in the front and back of the line can communicate.

> " Wheresoever you go, go with all your heart. "
>
> — **Confucius (551–479 BCE) Philosopher and teacher**

Working with Government

An important part of being socially active is being aware of your role as a citizen and your relationship with your government. This means understanding the problems and concerns of your community and how the policies of your government affect your community. As an active citizen, you must learn how to participate within your community and how to influence the government directly and effectively. When you stand up to have a say in your government, you are asserting your power to effect positive change.

Be prepared

Getting involved in social issues can sometimes lead to working with governments and government officials. Governments exist to serve the people they represent, so do not be afraid to speak out about issues that concern you. This is a big step. Be prepared. Do your research. Make sure that you understand the issue.

Since governments represent all of the people in a given area, you may have to demonstrate that a lot of people agree with you before the government will act on your suggestions. Part 2 examines in more detail some strategies you can use — such as surveys, petitions, and the media — to demonstrate that you have the support of many people.

Do not be afraid to attend public meetings and express your opinion

Your community may hold a meeting to discuss a bill or a community proposal (for example, close a library, turn a park into a parking lot, plant trees, and so on). This would be a great opportunity to express your opinion and have it on record. Others may be influenced by your words. Testifying as a witness is very much like making a speech. Refer to the section Public Speaking beginning on page 37 in Part 2 for some helpful tips.

Do not be afraid of criticism

Naturally, people's opinions on various issues differ. Some people may not agree with you, but do not be discouraged if this happens. Focus on your issue, and do not take any difference of opinion personally. Instead, try to learn from criticism you receive; it will make you and your work stronger.

Working with governments often involves influencing people and trying to convince them about the merit of your point of view. The more you know about your issue, the more effective your arguments will be and the more confident you will become.

Influencing Your Local Government

Your local government has jurisdiction over police, fire and ambulance services, parks, street cleaning, zoning by-laws, and public transit. Government decisions in these areas can affect you directly, and so there is a natural tendency to become most passionate about these types of issues. Rallying people to a local cause

and appealing to your local government has great potential for success and can result in changes that influence the daily life of your community.

Contact an elected official

Contact the elected official in your area and ask for her or his support. For instance, you may need help starting a youth council in your community, where young people would have a voice on issues that concern them. Or, you may want an elected official to draft and introduce a bill to support a particular cause. When you meet the official, be well prepared with facts and other information about your issue. Elected officials represent the people, but they are very busy; you need to get their attention and make your point quickly and strongly. Convincing them to work with you is the first step.

Let people know

Promote your cause by using the media and getting support from the community. Media coverage of an issue will help to influence the government. Create colorful posters and flyers and obtain permission, if necessary, to post them in high-traffic areas, such as the public library, the community center, and schools. You may also want to write a letter to the editor of your local newspaper. Try to

Tip

Influencing your government is serious business and it is quite natural to feel nervous about getting involved with government officials. But do not forget that you are a citizen and that your opinion counts. Take strength from the many other young people who have been in this same position and probably felt as you do now. Ask an adult or a friend to help you, if necessary.

WHERE YOU CAN GET INVOLVED— EVERYWHERE!

97

think of other ways you can get your message across to the greatest number of people. (Part 2 contains some additional ideas.) Be sure to provide an address where people can get in touch with you or your group for more information or to volunteer to help. The more people involved in your cause, the greater your chance of influencing your local government's position on an issue.

Organize a petition

Write a petition supporting the bill your elected official will be introducing on your behalf. This will help the official prove that there is plenty of community support for your idea, which will increase the chance of the bill becoming a law. Your petition should state the issue, say why it is important, and ask for the bill to be passed. Refer to the section How to Write a Petition beginning on page 46 in Part 2 for more specific instructions. Get as many signatures as you can, and then submit the petition to your elected official.

Other Ways to Get Involved with Government

There are many ways of getting involved with your government. You can research the structure of your government, become a student representative on a community youth council, work as a page in Congress, or volunteer in a campaign or on a council. These are all challenging and exciting ways of helping you understand how government works. Remember, knowledge is power. Once you have learned the system, you will have the power to influence the decisions it makes.

Learn about your system of government

- Visit your state legislature or your nation's capital to learn about government.

- Write to Congress requesting information about how the federal government works.

- Be familiar with your country's Constitution. Your library should have a copy of this document.

Become a student representative

- If your school does not have a student government, start one.

- Urge your Parent–Teacher Association (PTA) or student council to create a student representative position within the Association.

- Get involved in other organizations that might need and welcome a youth perspective.

TAKE ACTION!

Volunteer at your city councilor's office

- Volunteer to do any work you might find interesting. Do not be shy to ask what sorts of jobs there are, or suggest what you feel needs to be done.

- Volunteer for a state representative or congressman.

All of these activities will give you experience that will help you to understand how governments work and how you can influence them.

Lobby governments

Lobbying means applying pressure on governments to influence them to take a stand on an issue. It can involve writing letters, attending meetings, and writing petitions. You can do this at the municipal, state, or federal level.

What other ways can you think of to influence governments? What issues do you think need addressing? Here are a few examples:

- Ask for funds to be allocated for the building of a playground in your community.

- Ask for tough penalties for companies that harm the environment by dumping hazardous wastes or toxic chemicals into rivers.

- Ask governments to take a stand on child labor. You might ask your federal government to trade only with countries that have compulsory education for all children.

PART 4

Tackling Social Issues

Human Rights

On December 10, 1948, the General Assembly of the United Nations adopted and proclaimed the Universal Declaration of Human Rights. This document established that all people in the world have certain basic human rights, such as the right to food, simple housing, and political freedom, and that these rights should be protected and respected. The member states of the United Nations (nearly all the countries in the world) promised to uphold and enforce this important document.

Over half a century has passed since the Universal Declaration of Human Rights was introduced. What progress has been made during this time? Some people argue that very little has changed. Human rights abuses continue every day around the world. Here are just a few examples that outline ongoing or recent neglect of human rights:

- According to the United Nations, over two billion people survive on less than two dollars a day and the majority of them cannot afford even the most basic food, housing, or health care.

- Based on studies carried out by the World Bank, women around the globe perform two-thirds of the world's work, receive less than one-tenth of the world's income, and own less than one-one hundredth of the world's property.

- There are thousands of political prisoners in countries like China, Burma, and Turkey. Frequently, the crime that these people have committed has been simply to demand freedom of speech in their respective countries.

Clearly the issue of human rights is still an area that needs great attention. In order to uphold the Universal Declaration of Human Rights, everyone must help. One way that you can help is by organizing a Human Rights Awareness Day at your school. Education is the most important step in making this world a place where everyone's rights are respected.

Here are some other possibilities for action:

- Write letters to governments demanding that they protect human rights and link trade and economic development to human rights issues.

- Find out which major companies are human rights abusers. Research non-governmental organizations like Amnesty International and Human Rights Watch to find out which corporations have been linked to unfair labor practices. You may be surprised to find out which companies use sweatshop labor or child labor. Research a specific human rights abuser (a country or a company) and give a presentation to your class, student council, or local government. Education is the best way to stop human rights abuses.

What is the United Nations and what is its role?

The United Nations is an international organization made up of member countries that come together to discuss important world affairs. Over 180 countries, including the United States, belong to the United Nations. This body has helped to negotiate some very important international agreements, such as the United Nations Convention on Human Rights and the United Nations Convention on the Rights of the Child. Visit their Web site to obtain more information about the United Nations.

How to Organize a Human Rights Awareness Day

Choose your issue

Become enthusiastic about organizing a Human Rights Awareness Day in your school.

Do some research

Research human rights violations around the world. In particular, see if there are any human rights abusers in your area, as there are sweatshops even in the United States. Make sure that your information is reliable and up-to-date (see Step 2: Do Your Research beginning on page 4 in Part 1 for some helpful tips). You may want to contact an organization for help. Part 5 lists contact information for these organizations.

Get support from a teacher and your principal

Talk with your teacher or principal about the fact that you want to organize a Human Rights Awareness Day in your school. Tell them about the information you discovered during your research and explain why you feel it is important that your classmates learn about human rights.

Build a team

Speak to your friends at school and in your community about the Human Rights Awareness Day. Ask them to become involved. You may also want to ask some adults to help.

Call a meeting

Hold a meeting once you have a team in order to make a plan of action.

Make a plan of action

Here are a few considerations you will want to keep in mind:

✔ What issues would you like to address during the Human Rights Awareness Day?

✔ How do you want your event to be set up? Plan a schedule for the day.

✔ Would you like to invite guest speakers to your event? Which groups could you contact?

✔ When will the event be held? The date you choose should not conflict with any other events being held at the school.

• How will the Human Rights Awareness Day be publicized?

• Will local media be invited to cover the event? (See the section How to Use the Media beginning on page 51 in Part 2 for some helpful strategies.)

Take action and then review

Make your Human Rights Awareness Day a reality. Enjoy the day and have fun while learning more about important social issues. When the day is over, encourage everyone to continue learning about human rights issues.

Soon after the event, bring your team together to discuss what went well and what lessons were learned that the group can use to improve the next event. Thank everyone for participating.

Have fun!

Have fun while organizing the event, and enjoy spending time with your friends while participating in a worthwhile cause. Suggest a team activity to celebrate the successful organization of your Human Rights Awareness Day.

Profile: Elias Roman

Two years ago, Elias Roman began a chapter of Kids Can Free the Children at Friends Academy in Douglaston, New York. When he started the chapter he could not have predicted the tragedy of September 11th or the role his group would play. After the terrorist attacks, he and his KCFTC chapter asked, "Why did this happen, and what can *we do* about it?" They came up with an answer. Soon after asking that question, Elias and his friends began collecting supplies to send to the children of Afghanistan.

The group wanted to reach out, understanding that Afghan children were also suffering because of the tragedy. Innocent Afghani families were migrating to refugee camps, abandoning their homes for fear of retaliation. Elias and his friends figured out some of the basic things they knew displaced children in these camps would need. They modeled their efforts on the school and health kit campaign, and came up with "relief kits." They collected $100,000 worth of warm clothes, toothpaste, toothbrushes, bandages, and soap. They shipped their relief kits directly to the children of Northern Afghanistan. Kids Can Free the Children was able to work with one of its partner organizations, Counterpart International, to arrange the shipping and distribution of the goods for free.

The result was that Elias and his Kids Can Free the Children chapter were able to provide basic supplies to thousands of children who were affected by this conflict. The relief kits were a testament to the power of his group to come together and make a difference during this difficult time. The entire school community got behind this initiative and helped the group to make a real difference!

Children's Rights Are Human Rights

It is important for young people to understand their rights. In 1989, world leaders gathered together to determine the rights of children. The result was the United Nations Convention on the Rights of the Child. This is an international agreement that establishes the rights of children and young people who are under the age of 18. Over 190 countries around the world have accepted and have promised to enforce this important agreement. No other international human rights treaty has been more widely adopted on an international level.

The convention can be divided into four categories of rights.

1. **Playing a part:** This section of the agreement says young people must be included in the decision-making process on important issues that affect them. The document also says that young people have the freedom to join with other young people to protect their rights and to express their opinions.

2. **Reaching their potential:** This section of the agreement protects important social rights of youth. Included in this list are the right to have access to education and the right to protect their culture and identity.

3. **Living well: The right to survival:** This section of the agreement says that there are certain basic things that all young people must have, such as adequate food and shelter, a reasonable standard of living, and access to health care.

4. **Being free from harm:** This section of the agreement says that all young people should be protected from abuse, neglect, economic exploitation (child labor), torture, abduction (kidnapping and trafficking), and prostitution.

So far, however, the rights that were agreed upon in this important convention have yet to be upheld in some places. Right now, as you read this, millions of children around the world are being exploited and abused, while some governments continue to break their promises to take "all appropriate measures" to defend the rights of these young people.

All children deserve the right to be a kid and have their rights protected. The United Nations Convention on the Rights of the Child was a big step, but it was not enough. The good news is that you can help.

One way you can help children is by raising money to promote education in the developing world. Primary schooling is guaranteed under the United Nations Convention on the Rights of the Child, yet millions of children around the world do not have the opportunity to go to school because there are no educational resources in their communities. Education is the key to breaking the cycle of poverty and ending the exploitation of children. You will find out how to raise money to help children go to school below.

Some other possibilities for action include the following:

✔ Join an organization concerned with children's rights. See Part 5 for contact information.

✔ Write to your U.S. senator urging that he or she support the ratification of the United Nations Convention on the Rights of the Child. The United States is one of only two countries in the world that has not adopted this treaty. The other country is Somalia.

✔ Write letters and organize petitions to send to government officials to pressure them to make children's education a priority.

> "Thousands of candles can be lit from a single candle, and the life of the candle will not be shortened. Happiness is never decreased by being shared."
>
> — Buddha (c. 563–483 BCE) Philosopher and teacher

How to Raise Money to Help Children Go to School

Choose an issue

One in five of the world's children between the ages of six and eleven does not attend school. Become enthusiastic about joining the campaign to help children go to school.

Do some research

Research topics such as education, child labor, and child poverty (refer to Step 2: Do Your Research beginning on page 4 in Part 1 for some helpful tips). You may also want to contact Kids Can Free the Children for help. (See page 136 for contact information.)

Build a team

Involve your friends or give a presentation in front of your class about how education can put an end to the exploitation of children. Ask for their help. A group of people can raise money much more easily than you can by yourself.

Call a meeting

Speak to your friends at school and in your community about participating in raising money to help children go to school. Ask them to become involved and meet with you to make a plan of action. You may also want to ask some adults for their support.

Make a plan of action

Here are a few costs you may want to keep in mind.

- $1000 pays the salary of a teacher for a year in a developing country.

- $750 pays to put a concrete floor in a school.

- $200 buys a cow and feed or a small machine for a family as an alternative source of income so that children are freed from child labor and can go to school.

- $15 buys a desk for a child.

- $10 pays for a school kit for a child so he/she can have the tools to learn.

- With whom do you need to work to make your fundraiser successful?

- What materials will you need for your fundraiser? How many young people do you want to become involved in this campaign?

- Refer to the section 101 Fundraisers beginning on page 70 in Part 2 for fundraising suggestions.

- How will you advertise your fundraiser? Will you invite the media to your event?

You may even want to raise enough money to build a school in a developing country! Contact Kids Can Free the Children for detailed information.

Take action and then review

Make your fundraiser(s) a reality. Tell people about the event and why it is such a worthy cause. Make sure that people know how to contact you.

When your event is complete, send the money that you raised to Kids Can Free the Children, which will then send you information about the children and the community that you and your group helped. Share this information with all of the people who were involved in the fundraiser. Your supporters will then see the effect of their contribution and will be more likely to help in the future.

Soon after your event, bring your team together and discuss what aspects of the fundraiser were successful, as well as lessons the group learned that can be used to improve the next event.

Remember to thank everyone who participated in your event.

Have fun!

Have fun while organizing the event, and enjoy spending time with your friends while participating in a worthwhile cause.

Suggest a team activity to celebrate the hard work and dedication it took to contribute to the education of children in the developing world.

Profile: Chris Pettoni

Chris Pettoni is actively involved in Kids Can Free the Children's School Building Campaign, which promotes education for children in rural areas of developing countries. Chris was nine years old when he was first inspired to take action for children's rights. He attended a presentation given by Craig Kielburger on the exploitation of children around the world, and, very moved by what he learned, felt that he had to do something to help. By making presentations in his New Jersey school about Kids Can Free the Children and the issue of children's rights, Chris was able to motivate the students to establish a Free the Children committee and begin to fundraise for the School Building Campaign. By the end of the year, the team had raised over $3378, which was enough to build a school in Nicaragua, pay a teacher's salary for a year, and provide the new students with school supplies.

In October 1999, Chris was selected to represent his school on the Oprah Winfrey show, which was devoting an episode to children who were making a difference in the world. Chris was called out to present Craig Kielburger with a check for the money his school had raised. So impressed with the children's efforts, Oprah announced that she wanted to commit to building 50 schools in developing countries. "It was amazing to see our small school fundraiser reach out and touch so many people around the world," Chris said.

As Chris and his team continued to fundraise, they were able to pay for running water to be brought into a village in Nicaragua. The following year, Chris organized a school-supply drive to help several Kids Can Free the Children sponsored schools in South America that had been devastated by tropical storms. Now an active member of the Pompton Lakes, New Jersey, chapter of Kids Can Free the Children, Chris continues his work to promote and protect children's rights by speaking out and fundraising to help children go to school.

Environment

Earth is our home, and it is very important to protect it.

If we pollute the air and the water, we will harm the plants and animals of the world as well as ourselves. Everyone can make a contribution to preserving our environment by thinking about how our actions — such as how much garbage we throw away — affect the planet, and how adjusting our behavior might help to remedy the situation.

If there is an environmental issue that interests you, do some research to find out more about it. Consider these issues:

- water quality
- garbage
- CFCs (chlorofluorocarbons)
- acid rain
- soil erosion
- deforestation
- ozone layer
- greenhouse effect
- animal conservation
- wilderness preservation

These are all important and complicated issues. Our planet is in trouble and unless we take action, the damage could be irreversible. The good news is that you can help.

One way you can help is by organizing a garbage-free lunch, picnic, or outing, as described in this section. Here are some other possibilities for action:

✔ Invite guest speakers to talk to your school about environmental issues.

✔ Organize a tree-planting day.

✔ Plant a garden to grow your own vegetables.

✔ Start a compost pile.

✔ Promote a recycling program at your school.

✔ Organize a Clean Up the Park Day (make sure that you get permission from an adult and that there is adult supervision).

How to Organize a Garbage-Free Lunch

Choose an issue

Become enthusiastic about helping to protect the environment. Choose which area of the environment you would like to focus on, such as reducing the amount of garbage going into landfill sites.

Do some research

Find out why the 3Rs (reduce, reuse, recycle) are important and how a garbage-free lunch can help the environment. Also, find out how much garbage your school produces on an average day. Probably the best way to do this is to ask each class to keep track of how much garbage they throw away on any given day, or speak to your school's caretaker.

Think of some ways you can reduce the amount of garbage you produce in your school during lunchtime. For example:

✔ use reusable plastic containers instead of plastic wrap

✔ bring a sports bottle instead of a canned or boxed drink

✔ use a lunch box or thermal pack instead of a paper bag to carry your lunch

✔ avoid prepackaged convenience foods

Get support from a teacher and your principal

Talk to a teacher and your principal about the research you have done and about the importance of organizing a garbage-free lunch program. You may wish to involve an adult sponsor.

Build a team

Involve your friends or give a presentation in front of your class about the environment and about garbage-free lunches. Ask for their help. There is strength in numbers.

Call a meeting

Speak to your friends at school and in your community about participating in a Garbage-Free Lunch Day. Ask them to become involved and meet with you to make a plan of action. You may also want to ask some adults for help.

Make a plan of action

Address the following issues when you are organizing your garbage-free lunch:

• Should a letter be sent home to students' families explaining the Garbage-Free Lunch Day?

• If you have a cafeteria/dining hall in your school, is there some way you could involve it in your campaign?

- When will the campaign be held? The date you choose should not conflict with any other events being held at the school.
- How will you advertise the Garbage-Free Lunch Day? How much advance notice do you need to give to the school student body?
- How are you going to keep this project sustainable (keep it going after the one event)?

Take action and then review

Make your Garbage-Free Lunch Day a reality. Enjoy knowing that you have done something very valuable to help the environment.

Draw a chart comparing the amount of garbage thrown out on a typical day with the amount thrown out on a Garbage-Free Lunch Day. Post the chart in a high-traffic area of the school, and announce the results over the P.A. system. You will be amazed at the difference! When people understand that they can make a big difference by changing their own routine, they will be encouraged to make garbage-free lunches a habit.

Soon after the event, review with the team what went well and what was learned in order to make the next Garbage-Free Lunch Day an even greater success. Remember to thank everyone who helped you organize your event.

Have fun!

Enjoy knowing that your efforts have resulted in less waste being needlessly added to the tons of garbage produced every day. You have made a difference, so consider celebrating your contribution by organizing a team activity, such as going for a hike or camping in the natural environment you have helped to protect.

Profile: Melissa Poe

Melissa Poe is the founder of an organization called Kids for a Cleaner Environment (Kids FACE). She became an environmentalist at the age of nine, when what she learned about pollution moved her at once to take action to protect the environment. Melissa began by writing a letter to then President George Bush, asking him to address the issue of pollution more forcefully. Although his response ignored her concerns, Melissa was determined to make herself heard. She contacted a billboard company and convinced them to put a copy of her letter on 250 billboards.

Armed with creativity and resolve, Melissa made it known to President Bush and to adults everywhere that children cared about the environment and were ready to take a stand.

When she founded Kids FACE in 1989, the group had only six members. These young people sought to preserve the environment by recycling, picking up litter, and planting trees. Within a few years, however, Kids FACE had grown into the largest youth environmental organization in the world. The determination of a small group of young people was able to inspire children all over the world to take action in defence of the environment.

Melissa has become the spokesperson for the 100% Recycled Paperboard Alliance, encouraging people to buy products made from recycled paper with the slogan "Finish what you start." At the Global Earth Summit in Rio de Janeiro, Brazil, the most important environmental conference to date, Melissa was invited to speak again, as someone who played a significant role in making thousands of young people passionate about protecting their world.

Hunger

Hunger is one of the most important social issues facing the world today. About 40,000 people are dying every day from hunger-related illnesses. This is despite the fact that there is more than enough food currently produced on the planet to feed our current population. Clearly, this is not a matter of lack of resources. Food is always available to those who can afford to buy it.

Hunger is a complicated issue. There is no one reason why world hunger exists. Contributing factors include politics, distribution, economics, and production. Even though the United States and Canada are among the richer countries in the world, hunger is still a major North American problem. According to the Hunger Resource Centre, there are over 30 million hungry people in the United States, half a million hungry people in Canada, and an estimated 800 million hungry people in the world. You can help reduce this number.

One way that you can help is by organizing a Halloween for Hunger campaign. Instead of trick-or-treating for candy this coming October 31, collect food for your local food bank.

> "Hunger is the most degrading of adversities; it demonstrates the inability of existing culture to satisfy the most fundamental human necessities, and it always implies society's guilt.
>
> — Josué de Castro (1908–1973) Professor and advocate against world hunger

Here are some other possibilities for action:

✔ Do not waste food. Make sure to take only as much food as you are going to eat. This is something that everyone can work on.

✔ Organize a can drive through your school or place of worship.

✔ Organize a day of fasting (not eating) to raise awareness about hunger. You may want to participate in the 30-Hour Famine. Make sure that you have an adult advisor helping you, and that your parents/guardians are aware of what you are doing.

How to Organize a Halloween for Hunger Campaign

A Halloween for Hunger campaign involves collecting non-perishable food supplies at Halloween instead of candy. The canned goods can then be donated to local food banks to help people who are hungry.

Choose an issue

Become enthusiastic about helping the poor around the world who are hungry by organizing a Halloween for Hunger event.

Do some research

Find out about hunger in the United States, North America, and around the world. Visit Web sites such as that of Sports for Hunger for useful facts and statistics. Contact your local food bank to find out about hunger in your area.

Build a team

Involve your friends or give a presentation in front of your class about Halloween for Hunger. Ask if your fellow classmates want to become involved. If more people are part of your team, you will be able to collect more canned food for hungry people.

Call a meeting

Hold a meeting once you have a team in order to make a plan of action.

Make a plan of action

Here are some aspects of the campaign that you will want to keep in mind when developing your plan of action:

• Where will the food go once it is collected?

• People will need to be informed ahead of time that you will be collecting food instead of candy on Halloween. Put up flyers and posters around the community, informing people when you will be collecting and that you are looking for canned or non-perishable foods. One good idea is to put up a poster in or near grocery stores (ask for permission first).

- How will you transport all of the canned goods once they are collected? Will everyone meet in a central location to make sorting of the cans easier?

- Do you want to tell the local media about your campaign? Do you want to spread the campaign to other schools and other communities?

- You may want to figure out which neighborhood each volunteer will cover. After all, you do not want to be asking the same people twice and you do not want to miss anyone. Try mapping out the community and assign different streets or areas to individual volunteers.

- Remember, if you are going to houses of people you do not know, have an adult accompany you (and the adult can help carry the cans you collect).

Take action and then review

Make your Halloween for Hunger campaign a success. Collect the non-perishable food items while having fun dressing up in Halloween costumes. Feel good in

knowing that you are making a difference in the lives of others. Once the event is over, consider displaying posters to inform people in your community how much food was collected and to thank them for their contributions.

Soon after the event, review with your team what worked well and what could be improved the next time you conduct a similar campaign. What steps might be taken to sustain the campaign year-round?

Have fun!

A Halloween for Hunger event is intended to be fun. To bolster enthusiasm, consider hosting a party before your volunteers go trick-or-treating in the community.

Halloween for Hunger

Halloween for Hunger started with a small group of people who wanted to make a difference. Since then, the idea has spread so that now Halloween for Hunger collects millions of cans of food all over the world, even in countries that do not celebrate Halloween! Contact the local media about the food that you raised so that the idea can continue to spread.

Profile: Shagufta Pasta

For Shagufta Pasta, the day her life changed began as a day like any other. She had gone to the library to sign out a stack of books relating to global issues, and by chance picked up a slim volume on international debt. As she read about how the debt of poor countries deprives children of the food they need, and keeps millions of people bound to poverty, Shagufta was deeply moved to do something to help. A week later, Kids Can Change the World was born.

Shagufta founded Kids Can Change the World as a completely youth-run organization dedicated to the realization of children's rights worldwide through financial reform, and to the empowerment of youth to become active agents of change. Chapters are established at local schools where the organization leads workshops on how to change the world. Some of the means Kids Can Change the World uses to effect change include letter-writing campaigns; circulating petitions through schools and via on-line resources; creating and distributing information packages to educate teachers about debt and its impact on world hunger; and informing students about ways they can become more socially involved.

Shagufta's strong conviction that youth can change the world, that they are the most powerful way to create lasting change, is the spirit that drives Kids Can Change the World. Founding and shaping the organization has given Shagufta the opportunity to become a better leader, to develop new skills and talents, and ultimately, to inspire, lead, and become part of a dynamic and energetic group of people who are all working toward the same goals.

Poverty

Poverty is the one of the largest and most complex problems currently facing the world. The reason poverty is such a key area of concern is that it either causes or contributes to nearly all other social issues discussed in this book. For example, the environment is destroyed because poorer countries must sell their natural resources for sustenance. Similarly, one of the main reasons why children die of hunger or why they cannot go to school and receive an education is that they are poor.

Here are some statistics about poverty around the world:

- According to the World Bank Development Report of 1999/2000, 1.3 billion people (about one-quarter of the world's population) live in absolute poverty with incomes of less than $1 per day. Seventy percent of these individuals are women and children.

- According to the 1999 UNICEF State of the World's Children Report, to provide every child in the world with primary education for one year would cost approximately $10 billion.

- One out of every five North American children lives below the poverty line.

Education is the key to breaking the cycle of poverty

An education gives children the opportunity to have a better future. With the skills obtained through an education, children will be able to receive higher paying jobs (when they are older) and be better able to support their family. This will, in turn, enable their children to receive an education as well.

Many children around the world cannot attend school simply because they cannot afford to buy school supplies. Making school kits composed of basic school supplies can allow children to go to school for an entire year. Find out how to make school kits on the next page.

Here are some other ways you can act to combat poverty:

- ✔ Volunteer at your local homeless shelter.

- ✔ Encourage government officials through letter-writing campaigns to support legislation that will eliminate the debts of developing countries.

You may want to conduct a Web search to obtain information on the Jubilee Debt Campaign.

✔ Volunteer overseas by helping to build a school, dig a well to provide clean water, or teach English in a local primary school.

How to Make a School Kit

Choose an issue

Become enthusiastic about helping to create a more just and equitable world. Commit yourself to taking action by collecting school kits to send to children in developing countries.

Do some research

Research topics associated with education, such as child labor and child poverty. See Part 5 for some organizations you may want to research.

Build a team

Involve your friends or give a presentation in front of your class about the school kits campaign. Explain that there are many children who cannot go to school simply because they cannot afford basic school supplies. Ask if your classmates want to become involved. If more people are part of your team, you will be able to collect more kits.

Call a meeting

Hold a meeting once you have a team in order to make a plan of action on how you will organize your campaign.

Make a plan of action

Here are some questions to keep in mind when organizing your campaign:

✔ How will you obtain the needed supplies? Do you want to raise money and buy them? Do you want to put collection boxes around your school? Can the supplies be donated? The most common way is to have each student in the class bring in supplies to make one or two kits.

✔ Where will you store the kits until they are all collected?

✔ Will you need brochures or promotional materials to describe the campaign?

✔ How will you ship the supplies

School kits should include the following:

- 2 notebooks
- 1 ruler
- 6 pencils
- 2 erasers
- 1 pencil sharpener
- 1 pair of scissors
- 15 sheets of colored paper
- 1 box of crayons or colored pencils
- 1 tennis ball

Place these items in a cloth bag, preferably a canvas bag with handles that can be used as a school bag. You can contact Kids Can Free the Children once you have collected the supplies.

to their destination? Will you have to raise money for postage costs or can you get this service donated or sponsored?

Take action and review

Once you have gathered the supplies, assemble the kits and make sure they are complete. Once you have checked each kit, send them in a box to Kids Can Free the Children, which will then send the kits to needy children around the world.

Soon after your event, assemble your team to discuss any lessons the group learned that will make future campaigns even more successful. Be sure to discuss want went well and to thank everyone who helped make or deliver the kits.

Have fun!

Congratulate yourselves on making a difference by holding a pizza night to celebrate the campaign's success. Remind everyone who participated that even little items such as school supplies can make a huge difference in someone's life.

Profile: Audrey Ting

After attending a Kids Can Free the Children conference in the summer of 1999, Audrey Ting returned to Albany, New York, and helped start a chapter at Emma Willard High School. She had a new understanding of child labor and the poverty that forces many children to work to support their families. Audrey's chapter soon became involved with the New York State Labor Religion Coalition and with their "Sweat Free Schools" campaign. As the result of this campaign, all schools in the Albany area now ensure their school apparel is free of child labor.

After telling the stories of child laborers for a year and a half, Audrey decided she wanted to see what she was talking about firsthand. She wanted to tell the stories of children she had met herself.

She traveled in India for two weeks with KCFTC, in the summer of 2001. While in India, she did observe child labor firsthand. At different points during her trip she saw children weaving baskets, making jewelry, and rolling cigarettes for sale.

Audrey saw poverty from a different angle later on that same trip. She worked with physically challenged orphans at Mother Teresa's orphanage in Calcutta. She saw that these children needed her not only to feed and wash them, but also to provide love and caring. Those children were starving for affection as well as food.

Because Audrey believes that education is the lasting solution to breaking the cycle of poverty, she helped KCFTC build a school in one of the rural villages they visited. Although carrying the concrete to pour the foundation was hard work, Audrey was exhilarated by the excitement the new school had created in the village. The children who attended that school would not be weaving baskets, making jewelry, or rolling cigarettes for sale. The children attending school would be learning how to help themselves and their families avoid the cycle of poverty.

HIV/AIDS

HIV is a virus that destroys the body's capacity for immunity and results in AIDS. AIDS is a disease that is causing great concern around the world, in both developed and developing countries. There are over 34 million people infected with HIV/AIDS worldwide. Although progress has been made in caring for HIV/AIDS patients, there is no known cure. The AIDS virus is spreading particularly rapidly in developing countries. The main reason for the higher rates of infection in developing countries is a lack of education. Some of the leaders of developing countries even claim that the virus does not exist. One of the main reasons people get infected is simply that they do not realize that they are at risk.

How do people get infected?

Having unprotected sexual contact or sharing needles with an infected person causes the majority of the infections of HIV/AIDS. Also, mothers who have the disease can pass the illness on to their child before birth, during birth, or while breastfeeding. Blood transfusions can also cause infection, although this is extremely rare now due to blood screening. These are the only scientifically proven ways of contracting the HIV/AIDS virus.

Here are a few United Nations statistics about HIV/AIDS around the world:

- There were 5.3 million new infections in the year 2000 alone. More than 95% of these new infections were in developing countries.

- There were 3 million HIV/AIDS-related deaths in the year 2000. Of the people who died, five hundred thousand were children.

- Almost 22 million people in total have died as a result of HIV/AIDS. Over 4 million of these people were children.

- Over 13 million children have been orphaned because of HIV/AIDS. Many of these children end up in child labor because they often have no one to care for them or financially support them while they go to school.

On June 27, 2001, the Declaration on HIV/AIDS was approved by the United Nations General Assembly. This Declaration recognizes that HIV/AIDS is "a global crisis" and calls for "a global response." Essentially, this means that we all must work together to solve this problem. There are many things that you can do to help. One way is to organize an HIV/AIDS Awareness Day.

Here are some other possibilities for action:

- Raise money to give to organizations such as CARE and the National AIDS Fund. These organizations provide relief to AIDS patients and are involved in AIDS research.

- Write letters to major pharmaceutical companies (drug companies) telling them that you think they should provide AIDS medication to the developing world free of charge.

> "No act of kindness, no matter how small, is ever wasted."
>
> — Aesop
> (c. 620 B.C.)
> Author

How to Organize an HIV/AIDS Awareness Day

Choose an issue

Decide that you are passionate about joining the global campaign to rid the world of the HIV/AIDS virus and that you want to educate people about the disease through an HIV/AIDS Awareness Day.

Do some research

Obtain information about HIV/AIDS in your country and around the world. You can start at the Web sites for CARE and the National AIDS Fund. Make sure that your information is accurate and up-to-date.

Get support from a teacher and your principal

Talk to your teacher or principal about what you would like to do. Share what you discovered through your research and explain why you feel it is important that your classmates learn about this important social issue. You may also want to find a teacher to work with you.

Build a team

Make a presentation to your class about the HIV/AIDS Awareness Day. Share your research information and ask for volunteers to become involved in this event.

Call a meeting

Hold a meeting once you have a team in order to make a plan of action.

Make a plan of action

Consider the following when you are developing your plan of action:

- Think about how you want your event to be set up. Plan a schedule for the day.

- Would you like to invite guest speakers to your event? Which groups could you contact?

- Choose a date for the event that will not conflict with any other events that are being held at the school.

- Determine ways to publicize the HIV/AIDS Awareness Day.

the HIV/AIDS Awareness Day in order to improve next year's event.

Do not forget to thank everyone who was involved.

Take action and then review

Have a successful and educational HIV/AIDS Awareness Day. When the day is over, encourage everyone to continue learning more about the issue of HIV/AIDS.

Soon after the event, review the strengths and weaknesses of

Have fun!

Have fun while organizing the event and enjoy spending time with your friends while participating in such a worthwhile cause. Suggest a fun activity that you and your team can do to celebrate a great HIV/AIDS Awareness Day.

Profile: Nkosi Johnson

CP Picture Archive
(Themba Hadebe)

Nkosi Johnson, a 12-year-old African, was called "the courageous boy who moved a continent" for helping to break the silence about HIV and AIDS. He inspired millions of people around the world by being open about his disease in a country where families and communities often shun people with AIDS. Nkosi's own mother had been forced to abandon him when he was two because she had been ostracized by her neighbors for being HIV-positive.

In 1997, Nkosi and his foster mother, Gail Johnson, successfully challenged a public primary school that refused to admit him because he had HIV. Their fight led to a policy forbidding schools from discriminating against HIV-positive children, and to guidelines for how schools should treat infected students.

Nkosi spoke out to raise AIDS awareness and challenged people to re-examine their fear of people with AIDS. He attracted worldwide attention when he spoke in July 2000 at the 13th International AIDS Conference in the South African city of Durban, asking for compassion for AIDS victims and urging the government to provide HIV-positive pregnant women with drugs to prevent the transmission of the virus to their infants. Nkosi became a symbol of courage in the face of AIDS, and before he lost his life to the disease on June 1, 2001, he used his fame to raise money for Nkosi's Haven, a shelter for HIV-positive mothers and their children. "It is a great pity that this young man has died, he was very bold," said former South African President Nelson Mandela, who has called Nkosi an "icon of the struggle for life."

Source: Adapted from: Susanna Loof, "Nkosi Johnson, 12, Dies; S. African AIDS Activist: Boy Born With HIV Urged Openness," The Washington Post. Saturday, June 2, 2001; pg. B07

Peace

Our history books are filled with stories of war, and even though we tend to study wars and famous battles, we very rarely celebrate and study peace. One of the reasons the issue of peace is so urgent today is that we live in an age of nuclear weapons. Nuclear weapons are so powerful that it is possible to destroy all of humanity and even Earth itself with only the touch of a button. Nuclear weapons have made war even more dangerous than in the past.

Along with nuclear weapons comes a new possibility of peace. Previously, it was believed that the mere threat of a potential nuclear war would be enough to encourage governments to work together and to commit themselves to peace. But clearly their priorities have not yet evolved in this direction.

Here are some facts on military spending:

- The world currently spends $800 billion dollars on military expenditures each year.

- There are over 30,000 nuclear weapons in the world today. This represents enough nuclear warheads to destroy the world 10 times over.

- The world spends more money on the military than on anything else by far. In fact, according to the Nuclear Age Peace Foundation, a mere 30% of the global military budget would be enough money to solve nearly all of the world's problems, including hunger, illiteracy, and many environmental issues.

Our world does not have to be constantly at war. Real peace is possible, but we must work together. There are many ways you can help. One way is by organizing a War Is Not a Game campaign in your school or community. The War Is Not a Game campaign encourages people to boycott war toys. The purpose of this campaign is to help people realize that while some children play war, many children actually fight in wars as child soldiers. This campaign raises awareness not only about the exploitation of children, but also about the importance of peace.

Here are some other possibilities for action:

- Start a Nuclear Age Peace Foundation chapter in your school. Contact their Web site and request a chapter start-up kit.
- Write to your government officials and encourage them to promote peace and to support nuclear disarmament.
- Hold a Peace Day at your school to celebrate peace heroes like Nelson Mandela, the Dalai Lama, Mother Teresa, and Mahatma Gandhi.

> "The calamity of war, wherever, whenever, and upon whomever it descends, is a tragedy for the whole of humanity."
>
> — Raisa Gorbachev (1932–1999) Academic and former first lady of the Soviet Union

How to Organize a War Is Not a Game Campaign

Choose an issue

Become enthusiastic about creating a more peaceful world and commit yourself to organizing a War Is Not a Game campaign in your school.

Do some research

Gain more knowledge on the issue and learn about child soldiers, global military spending, and nuclear weapons. Visit the Web site of the Nuclear Age Peace Foundation as a starting point. Make sure the information you obtain is accurate and up-to-date.

Get support from a teacher and your principal

Talk to a teacher or your principal about the fact that you want to organize a War Is Not a Game campaign in your school. Demonstrate what you discovered through your research and explain why you feel it is important that your classmates learn about this important social issue.

Build a team

Make a presentation to your class about war and the sub-issues of nuclear weapons and children in armed conflict. Share your

research information and request the help of volunteers.

Call a meeting

Hold a meeting once you have a team in order to develop a plan of action.

Make a plan of action

Keep in mind the following points when making your plan of action:

- Investigate whether or not your local toy stores carry war toys. If they do sell them, tell them about the campaign and why you feel that it is important. You may be able to convince them to stop selling war toys. If they do not carry war toys, ask them if you can put up a sign about the campaign in their window. Also, encourage people to buy from their store to reward them for their moral position.

- How will you publicize the campaign?

- Will you need brochures or extra information to educate people about the issue?

- Can you organize an event for the first day of your campaign that will launch the initiative? If so, what will this event consist of? Do you need any guest speakers?

- If you decide to collect old war toys from your friends and family, how will you organize this part of the campaign?

- Will you contact the media? What will be your message? See the section How to Use the Media beginning on page 51 in Part 2 for helpful hints.

Take action and then review

Take action and have a successful War Is Not a Game campaign.

War Is Not a Game

War Is Not a Game is a global movement to boycott the buying and selling of war toys. The best time to launch this campaign is during the holiday period when people, usually parents, buy toys for young people. This undertaking usually involves:

- educating people about the campaign and the issue of war conflict through pamphlets, brochures, and the media

- getting friends and classmates to collect their old war toys in a number of boxes and, in a gathering of your school, educate the audience about the issue. This is followed by disposal of the old toys.

You can obtain more information about this campaign on the Kids Can Free the Children Web site.

Educate people about creating a safer world using the example of war toys.

Soon after the event, bring your team together and discuss the good points of the campaign, as well as some lessons that the group has learned in order to make a similar event even better next time.

Make sure you thank everyone involved in the campaign.

Have fun!

Have fun while taking part in this worthwhile campaign, and then celebrate your team's success after it is over.

Profile: Sadako Sasaki

Sadako Sasaki was a young girl with a dream of peace. She survived the atomic bomb attack at Hiroshima in 1945, but 10 years later she developed leukemia because of the radiation produced by the nuclear explosion. While she was struggling with the disease, she was reminded of the Japanese legend of the paper crane. It was believed that constructing 1,000 paper cranes would protect anyone from illness. Sadako began making her cranes with the hope of returning to health. As she said, "I will write peace on your wings and you will fly all over the world." Unfortunately, she was only able to make 644 paper cranes before she died in 1955.

Her classmates folded the remaining 356 cranes and raised money to build a monument commemorating the thousands of children who lost their lives because of the nuclear bomb. The monument is a statue of Sadako holding a paper crane in her outstretched hand. The base of the statue reads:

> This is our cry
> This is our prayer
> Peace in the world

Sadako Sasaki has inspired many people to dedicate their lives to working for peace. Even now, many years after her death, she continues to do so. Every year, people send thousands of paper cranes to be placed at the base of her statue in the hope of peace.

More Issues for Social Action

Choose an issue that moves you, do your research, and get involved. What follows are several ideas that might inspire you.

Help to free political prisoners

Write letters to world leaders asking them to free political prisoners. There are thousands of people around the world who have been jailed because they believe in democracy and freedom of speech. You can contact Amnesty International through their Web site in order to obtain more information about writing letters to help free political prisoners. You can also refer to the section Writing Letters beginning on page 25 in Part 2 of this book.

Help homeless people

Volunteer at a soup kitchen or a local food bank. You can also make an I Care kit for a homeless person that includes food, a sleeping bag, and some warm clothes. You may want to join a community group to help find long-term solutions for the homeless.

Organize a "buy nothing" day

The world is becoming increasingly materialistic. Particularly in North America, people are encouraged to buy more and more consumer goods. Individuals sometimes tend to forget that happiness is not defined by how many material possessions one owns. One really good way of reminding people of this fact is to organize a day during which classmates, friends, and family buy nothing. This will help them realize that there are more important things in life than possessions.

Sweatshops

Sweatshops are places where workers are forced to work long hours in inhumane conditions for very little pay. Usually the people who work in sweatshops are women or children. Become informed about the conditions that sweatshop workers endure.

Initiate or join campaigns organized in response to these conditions; take action to support the struggle of sweatshop workers for better conditions and wages. You are not powerless to help.

> "Individual advances turn into social change *when enough of them occur.*"
>
> — **Elizabeth Janeway (b. 1913) Writer**

Start in your own school. Find out if any school materials are manufactured using sweatshop labor by requesting source information on where your school buys its products. Gather a group of supporters and pressure your school board to buy only from manufacturers that provide their employees with just working conditions and do not employ children. You can do this by demanding that companies provide you with a code of ethics, which you can review.

Diversity

Our world is filled with so many wonderfully different cultures, colours, and languages. Such diversity gives us the continuous opportunity to learn and make new discoveries. Many people, however, look at differences in terms of negatives, which often results in racial conflicts. You can encourage people to appreciate differences and to promote tolerance. Start up a Diversity Club at your school. Organize an assembly that highlights different cultural performances. Talk to your school board about including a broader range of ideas and values in your school's curriculum.

Educate youth about drugs and alcohol

Educate your classmates and friends about the danger of drugs and alcohol. Conduct research to find statistics and to learn about the effects of drugs and alcohol. You can give a presentation in front of your class. Starting an after-school club that provides drug-free activities is another great possibility.

PART 5

Sources and Resources

There are many organizations you will find to be valuable as you explore issues that are important to you. The following list is only a starting point.

Human Rights

Amnesty International — USA

322 8th Avenue
New York, NY 10001
Tel: 212-807-8400
Fax: 212-463-9193 or
    212-627-1451
Email: admin-us@aiusa.org
Web site: www.aiusa.org

Human Rights Watch

350 Fifth Avenue, 34th floor
New York, NY 10118-3299
Tel: 212-290-4700
Fax: 212-736-1300
Email: hrwnyc@hrw.org
Web site: www.hrw.org

Office of the United Nations High Commissioner for Human Rights

Department of Public
    Information
Development and Human Rights
    Section
United Nations, Room S-1040
New York, NY 10017
Tel: 212-963-3771
Fax: 212-963-1186
Email: vasic@un.org
Web site: www.unhcr.ch

Children's Rights

The Children's Defense Fund

25 E Street NW
Washington, DC 20001
202-628-8787
Email: cdfinfo@childrensdefense
    .org
Web site: www.childrensdefense
    .org

Defence for Children International

1350 Sycamore Drive
Burlington, Ontario L7M 1H2
Tel + Fax: 905-319-0615
Canada
Email: les.horne2@sympatico.ca
Web site: www.defence-for-
    children.org

Kids Can Free the Children

50 High Oak Trail
Richmond Hill, Ontario L4E 3L9
Canada
Tel: 905-760-9382
Fax: 905-760-9157
E-mail: info@freethechildren.com
Web site: www.freethechildren
    .org

UNICEF — USA

UNICEF House
3 United Nations Plaza
New York, NY 10017
Tel: 212-326-7000
Fax: 212-887-7465 or
    212-887-7454
Email: netmaster@unicef.org
Web site: www.unicef.org

Environment

Defenders of Wildlife

National Headquarters
1101 14th Street, NW #1400
Washington, DC 20005
Tel: 202-682-9400
Fax: 202-682-1331
Email: info@defenders.org
Web site: www.defenders.org

Environmental Defense National Headquarters

257 Park Avenue South
New York, NY 10010
Tel: 212-505-2100
Fax: 212-505-2375
Email: Contact@
    environmentaldefense.org.
Web site: www
    .environmentaldefense.org

National Environmental Trust

1200 18th Street NW,
5th Floor
Washington, DC 20036
Tel: 202-887-8800
Fax: 202-887-8877
E-mail: netinfo@environet.org
Web site: www.environet.org

National Wildlife Federation

11100 Wildlife Center Drive
Reston, VA 20190-5362
Tel: 703-438-6000
Web site: www.nwf.org

Sierra Club

85 Second Street, Second Floor
San Francisco, CA 94105-3441
Tel: 415-997-5500
Fax: 415-997-5799
Email: information@sierraclub
.org
Web site: www.sierraclub.org

World Wildlife Fund — USA

1250 Twenty-Fourth Street, NW
P.O. Box 97180
Washington, DC 20090-7180
Tel: 1-800-CALL-WWF
Fax: 202-293-9211
Web site: www.worldwildlife.org

Hunger

Action Against Hunger — USA

875 Avenue of the Americas,
Suite 1905
New York, NY 10001
Tel: 212-967-7600
Fax: 212-967-5480
Email: aah@aah-usa.org
Web site: www.aah.org

Food First: Institute for Food and Development Policy

398 60th Street
Oakland, CA 94618
Tel: 510-654-4400
Fax: 510-654-4551
Email: foodfirst@foodfirst.org
Web site: www.foodfirst.org

Freedom from Hunger

1644 DaVinci Court
Davis, CA 95616
Tel: 800-708-2555
Fax: 530-758-6241
Email: info@freefromhunger.org
Web site: www.freefromhunger
.org

The Hunger Project — USA

15 E. 26th Street, #1401
New York, NY 10010
Tel: 212-251-9100
Fax: 212-532-9785
Email: info@thp.org
Web site: www.thp.org

Save the Children

54 Wilton Road
Westport, CT 06880
Tel: 1-800-728-8843
Web site: www.savethechildren
.org

World Hunger Education Service

3035 Fourth Street, NE
P.O. Box 29056
Washington, DC 20017
Tel: 202-269-6322
Fax: 202-269-1027
Email: hungernotes@aol.com
Web site: www.worldhunger.org

World Hunger Year

505 Eighth Avenue, Suite 2100
New York, NY 10018-6582
Tel: 212-629-8850
Fax: 212-465-9274
Email: WHY@world
hungeryear.org
Web site: www.worldhungeryear
.org

Poverty

ActionAid USA

1112 16th Street NW, Suite 540
Washington DC 20036-4823
Tel: 202-835-1240
Fax: 202-835-1244
Email: office@actionaidusa.org
Web site: www.actionaid.org

Coalition on Human Needs

1120 Connecticut Avenue N.W.,
    Suite 910
Washington, DC 20036
Tel: 202-223-2532
Fax: 202-223-2538
Email: chn@chn.org
Web site: www.chn.org

National Center for Children in Poverty

Mailman School of Public Health
    of Columbia University
154 Haven Avenue
New York, NY 10032
Tel: 212-304-7100
Fax: 212-544-4200
E-mail: nccp@columbia.edu
Web site: cpmcnet.columbia
    .edu/dept/nccp

NetAid

267 Fifth Avenue
11th Floor
New York, NY 10016
Phone: 212-537-0500
Fax: 212-537-0501
Email: info@netaid.org
Web site: www.netaid.org

OneWorld — USA

Benton Foundation
950 18th Street, NW
Washington, DC 20006
Tel: 202-638-5770
Fax: 202-638-5771
Email: us@oneworld.net
Web site: www.oneworld.net

Oxfam America

26 West Street
Boston, MA 02111
Tel: 1-800-77-oxfamusa
Fax: 617-728-2594
Email: info@oxfamamerica.org
Web site: www.oxfamamerica.org

RESULTS

440 First Street NW, Suite 450
Washington, DC 20001
Tel: 202-783-7100
Fax: 202-783-2818
Email: results@resultsusa.org
Web site: www.resultsusa.org

The United States Agency for International Development

US Agency for International
    Development Information
    Center
Ronald Reagan Building
Washington, DC 20523-1000
Tel: 202-712-4810
Fax: 202-216-3524
Email: pinquiries@usaid.gov
Web site: www.usaid.gov

The World Bank

Headquarters — General
    Inquiries
The World Bank
1818 H Street NW
Washington, DC 20433 USA
Tel: 202-477-1234
Fax: 202-477-6391
Email: feedback@worldbank.org
Web site: www.worldbank.org

World Vision United States

P.O. Box 9716
Federal Way, WA 98063-9716
Tel: 1-888-511-6598
Email: info@worldvision.org
Web site: www.worldvision.org

HIV/AIDS

CARE

151 Ellis Street
Atlanta, GA 30303
Tel: 404-681-2552
Fax: 404-589-2651
Email: info@care.org
Web site: www.care.org

Family Health International

P.O. Box 13950
Research Triangle Park,
    NC 27709
Tel: 919-544-7040
Fax: 919-544-7261
Email: skhalaf@fhi.org
Web site: www.fhi.org

National AIDS Fund

1030 15th St., NW, Suite 800
Washington, DC 20005
Tel: 202-408-4848 or
    1-888-234-AIDS
Email: info@aidsfund.org
Web site: www.aidsfund.org

UNAIDS

20, avenue Appia
CH-1211 Geneva 27
Switzerland
Tel: (+4122) 791-3666
Fax: (+4122) 791-4187
E-mail: unaids@unaids.org
Web site: www.unaids.org

The World Health Organization

525 23rd Street NW
Washington, DC 20037
Tel: 202-974-3000
Fax: 202-974-3663
Email: postmaster@paho.org
Web site: www.who.int

Peace

Abolition 2000: A Global Network to Eliminate Nuclear Weapons

PMB 121
1187 Coast Village Road,
    Suite #1
Santa Barbara, CA 93108-2794
Tel: 805-965-3443
Fax: 805-568-0466
Email: admin@abolition2000.org
Web site: www.abolition2000.org

The Association of World Citizens

55 New Montgomery Street,
    Suite 224
San Francisco, CA 94105
Tel: 415-541-9610
Fax: 650-745-0640
Email: info@worldcitizens.org
Web site: www.worldcitizens.org

NGO Committee on Disarmament

777 United Nations Plaza,
    Suite 3b
New York, NY 10017
Tel: 212-687-5340
Fax: 212-687-1643
Email: disarmtimes@igc.apc.org
Web site: www.igc.org/disarm

Nuclear Age Peace Foundation

PMB 121
1187 Coast Village Road, Suite 1
Santa Barbara, CA 93108-2794
Tel: 805-965-3443
Fax: 805-568-0466
Email: wagingpeace@napf.org
Web site: www@wagingpeace.org

Peace Action

1819 H Street NW, Suites 420 &
    425
Washington, DC 20006
Tel: 202-862-9740
Fax: 202-862-9762
Web site: www.peace-action.org

Seeds of Peace

370 Lexington Avenue, Suite 401
New York, NY 10017
Tel: 212-573-8040
Fax: 212-573-8047
Email: info@seedsofpeace.org
Web site: www.seedsofpeace.org

United States Institute of Peace

1200 17th St., NW, Suite 200
Washington, DC 20036-3011
Tel: 202-429-3842
Fax: 202-429-6063
Email: usip-requests@usip.org
Web site: www.usip.org

Women's International League for Peace and Freedom

1213 Race Street
Philadelphia, PA 19107
Tel: 215-563-7110
Fax: 215-563-5527
Email: wilpf@wilpf.org
Web site: www.wilpf.org

The World Institute for Non-Violence and Reconciliation

P.O. Box 352
Kingston, 7050
Tasmania, Australia
Tel: Australia - 03 6227 1494
International - 61 3 6227 1494
Fax: Australia - 03 6227 1520
International - 61 3 6227 1520
Email: aalomes@institute-for-
    nonviolence.com.au
Web site: institute-for-
    nonviolence.com.au

About Leaders Today

Leaders Today was founded by Marc and Craig Kielburger, who shared a vision to empower young people to become leaders of today in their schools, communities, and the world at large. Profits made through Leaders Today support the projects of the charitable organization, Kids Can Free the Children, and leadership programs for youth around the world.

Leaders Today offers the following unique and inspirational programs:

Volunteer opportunities

Leaders Today offers exciting volunteer opportunities at a local, national, and international level. It sponsors "volunteer days" in communities and schools and provides research materials to young people on social issues in which they can become involved.

Global leadership seminars

Trained facilitators from Leaders Today visit schools, places of worship, and community organizations administering one-, two-, or five-day leadership workshops.

Summer leadership programs in Africa, Central America, India, and Thailand

These programs provide young people with the unique opportunity to combine leadership training and volunteer experience with exposure to another culture and its people and landmarks. Trip highlights often include building a primary school, working with the children in a rural community, or volunteering at a medical clinic. A life-changing program for all those who participate!

Summer leadership academy

Located in Toronto, this program consists of an intensive one-week leadership training program. Participants learn how they can unleash their inner potential and passion to make a real and lasting difference in the world.

Become part of a Leaders Today program! Engage in leadership, volunteer in a meaningful way, and help change the world.

For more information about Leaders Today, please contact:
Leaders Today
50 High Oak Trail
Richmond Hill, Ontario L4E 3L9
Canada
www.leaderstoday.com

About Kids Can Free the Children

Kids Can Free the Children (KCFTC) is an international network of children helping children through representation, leadership, and action. It is an organization by, of, and for children. It works not only to free children from exploitation and abuse, but also to free children from the idea that they are powerless to effect positive change in the word and to improve the lives of their peers.

Kids Can Free the Children offers the following projects and activities:

School building campaign

Education is the best way to end the exploitation of children. KCFTC funds go toward paying for teachers' salaries, buying desks for classrooms, and helping to build schools.

School & health kit campaign

KCFTC has provided over 100,000 school and health kits to children in need, helping them to get an education and to stay healthy.

Anti–child labor campaign

KCFTC lobbies world governments and businesses to end sweatshop labor and child labor, builds rescue homes for children, and provides alternative sources of income for poor families.

War-affected children project

KCFTC is working with the United Nations to launch a campaign to help protect and assist children in situations of armed conflict. KCFTC is building a children-to-children network around the issue of children and war. KCFTC programs include the War Is Not A Game Campaign, the Children Paint Their Dreams Campaign, and Leadership Academies for Peace.

Anti–child poverty campaign

KCFTC campaigns world leaders to eliminate the debt in poor countries and has developed the Halloween For Hunger event.

For more information about KCFTC, please contact:
Kids Can Free the Children
50 High Oak Trail
Richmond Hill, Ontario L4E 3L9
Canada
www.freethechildren.com